THE LIFE AND TIMES OF
ST ANDREWS

'It stands by the sea, laid out in parallel lines of roads, with a noble surrounding of rich glebe, a place of lordly wealth; while the old lustre of the pontiffs remained, 'twas here the pontiff's mitre gleamed. It displays a palace of the Muses towering heavenward, the delight of gods and men. Here is the shady grove of Phoebus, here the sister Nymphs, with fair Urania the brightest of the throng. Here find I welcome on my return from the distant shores of the German, and am set in high place. A town happy beyond words, did it know the good gifts of the Muses, and the blessed realms of the god of heaven. Bountiful Creator, drive from the town evil plagues, and all things hurtful to the Muses; let Peace and Religion join hands.'

Poemata, Professor John Johnstoun (1570–1612), of
St Mary's College.

The Life and Times of
St Andrews

RAYMOND LAMONT–BROWN

Foreword by
FRANK MUIR

JOHN DONALD PUBLISHERS LTD
EDINBURGH

ISBN 0 85976 236 X

Phototypeset by Pioneer Associates (Graphic) Ltd., Perthshire.
Printed in Great Britain by Bell & Bain Ltd., Glasgow.

Foreword

I was never much a believer in magic but being Lord Rector of St Andrews University for three wholly enjoyable years changed all that.

When I first collected the hire car from Edinburgh airport and drove up the motorway to the Kingdom of Fife I was given a presage of what was to come: one always makes a mental note to watch out for the motorway exit number which is one before the one you want to leave by, so that you can slow down and move to the slow lane. The Exit which I had to leave by to get to St Andrews was Exit 8 so I kept my eyes peeled for the arrival of Exit 7. On the motorway north from Edinburgh there was then no Exit 7. You could get *on* the motorway at junction 7 if you were driving south but you could not get *off* it when you were driving north. I braked sharply as I suddenly and unexpectedly arrived at Exit 10 and mentally decided that the Scottish elves must have stolen Exit 7 for some personal use. As a runway for an experimental jet-propelled super-elf?

And then there was the matter of the St Andrews' Disappearing Street. When I arrived, I parked the car at the Students' Union and took a gentle stroll towards the harbour, looking about me. There were — I counted — three main thoroughfares, South Street, Market Street and North Street. But when I reached the far end of North Street I found that there were only two streets left. One of them had mysteriously evaporated en route. Surely the work of local goblins.

St Andrews had many more magical moments. For instance, the seemingly modest stone houses turned out to be three times bigger on the inside than they were on the outside. And what on earth became of the Star Hotel in

Market Street? I always used to stay there when I was Rector (my room, no 8, had an enormous nineteen-thirties-style washbasin, like the console of a Wurlitzer organ) but when I returned to St Andrews some years later the hotel had completely disappeared. Spirited away?

I always thought at the time that the secrets behind St Andrews' strange enchantments must lie somewhere in the history of the town — in its essential Scottishness, perhaps, or its learning — if only someone was prepared to dig deeply into its long and complicated past.

And that is just what Raymond Lamont-Brown, my old friend from many a town and gown occasion those many years ago, has done on your behalf. He has dug into archives, and walked St Andrews' wynds, and explored, and read tomes, for ten long years, and you are holding the result in your hands.

If you are interested, and everybody should be, in the history of this most individual, charming and beautiful of all wee Scottish towns then, as somebody once wrote (or was it perhaps a Kingdom of Fife literary imp?), 'Here be riches'.

Frank Muir

Preface

This volume is the end product of over a decade of study of, and residence in, St Andrews. It is dedicated to all who love the town and wish to see it flourish. The contents are a personal selection and perspective of the ancient burgh, and although it is the fruit of countless conversations with St Andreans from town and gown — particularly my friends in the St Andrews Preservation Trust, and the University of St Andrews — it remains an individual assessment.

It is my wish to thank all who have encouraged the work as it has proceeded and particularly John Tuckwell and Donald Morrison of John Donald Publishers Ltd who gave me the opportunity of writing the book about the town that plays such a part in my life and thoughts. I thank them too for their selection of pictures to go with my text; in commissioning some new ones and choosing several much-loved 'classics' which are individually acknowledged. My 'Further Reading' list reflects the authors past and present who have inspired my own research and I pay full tribute to them. And I extend a particular thanks to Dr Frank Muir for his kindness in supplying a Foreword to the book.

St Andrews   RAYMOND LAMONT-BROWN
1989

Contents

CHAPTER 1

From the Dawn of History

Over the hills they came and through the forests and across the marshes. Some were in groups, others were solitary horsemen, while a few huddled in family carts, but they all had a single purpose. These medieval pilgrims wended their sacred way into St Andrews led by the roads and tracks of North East Fife to the cathedral wherein was set their goal, the shrine of the Holy Martyr and Apostle Andrew of Bethsaida in Galilee. Today the successors of these pilgrims travel the new roads — the A91 from Cupar, the A918 and A959 from Crail and Anstruther, the A915 from Leven and the B939 from Ceres — to the modern shrine in the form of St Andrews golf courses. For St Andrews remains a place of purposeful travel, rather than somewhere to 'pass through'. The town stands as an enclave within Fife, a wedge of land beset on two sides by the North Sea, while on the other two lies an ocean of farmland. It is a sanctuary from man's industrial toils that have ravaged the west of the county, but here in St Andrews man first settled and left his mark.

To look enquiringly at the work of the earliest recorded inhabitants of the area we now know as St Andrews, the curious have to visit the museum set within the thirteenth century warming-house of the cathedral's priory precinct. For there rests in splendour the ancient artifact known as the St Andrews Sarcophagus, which experts believe is one of the finest examples of Dark Age art. It is indeed likely that this late eighth or early ninth century relic was a shrine rather than a coffin, although it forms a stone bier-like box made up of slabs slotted into corner-posts. Its gabled roof is entirely conjectural, but it is the earliest piece of surviving sculpture in St Andrews and is maybe all that is left of an earlier eighth

1

century church whose traces were finally destroyed during the wicked days of the Reformation. Once, the box had four thin sandstone panels fitted into four carved corner-posts. Only two of the panels and three of the posts survive, but the eye is drawn to the vigorous high relief of the carved hunting scene, which impressed scholars like C. A. Ralegh Radford who in 1955 assessed it as being a prominent example of the iconography of David the shepherd boy, slayer of Goliath and composer-collector of many of the psalms and who became Israel's second king and founded the royal line from which the Messiah was eventually born: Radford saw David herein 'as a prefiguration of Christ'.

The large figure on the sarcophagus's front panel is David rending the jaws of the lion as recorded in *I Samuel xvii. 35,* and a warrior on horseback wields a sword in his right hand and holds a falcon in his left while he is being attacked by a lion (maybe a depiction of the phrase from *II Timothy iv, 17*); underneath a standing figure carries shield and sword and is thought to have been inspired by the quote *Salve me ex ore leonis* ('Save me from the lion's mouth') of *Psalms, xii.21.* The figures are all dressed in costume which predates the customary Pictish dress. The artist of this sarcophagus, which was found in a deep grave in 1833 near St Rule's Tower, interlaced exotic beasts in his depiction; a griffon for instance, that beloved beast of medieval legend, half lion — half eagle, devours a mule and there are monkeys capering on the end panel. The St Andrews Sarcophagus has been whimsically surmised as being the coffin for the body of St Rule, who comes into the St Andrews story later. Incidentally, St Leonard's School, Pends Road, is in possession of a further 'shrine' (known as the St Leonards Shrine), discovered in 1895 when the foundations of St Rule's dormitory residence were being dug. It is a solid piece of stone handtooled as a 'house' shrine with Latin crosses and was found among long cists containing human remains.

In the cathedral museum, too, are pieces of early Christian sculptured stones all found nearby, which scholars believe link St Andrews with eighth to tenth century Northumbria wherein St Andrews was the centre of an important school and workshop of Celtic-Anglian art and a culture that faded away before the coming of the Norman prelates. But even these relics are young, for thousands of years before David was carved out of the sandstone, men dug and scraped and carved on St Andrews headland.

Some 10,000 years ago, the glaciers of the last Ice Age melted and plants began to colonise the land, followed by grazing animals and meat-eating predators including early man. People first came to the St Andrews area around 8000 BC; they came from the south and from across the North Sea, travelling by sea coast and river to penetrate the Kinness Burn and the Eden estuary, the earliest form of transport on water being the log boat. These peoples were hunter-gatherers who existed mainly on deer, wild cattle, birds, fish and shellfish, nuts, berries, roots and leaves. One early site, recently excavated, was Morton, once an island but now on the Tentsmuir peninsula. The first inhabitants, then, were a nomadic people who acquired the knowledge of food production around 4500 BC from the people who moved east from Europe. Farmers began to replace the hunters, and slowly a trade in stone axes was established and there was a development of pottery. Around 2500 BC a people came from Northern Europe who brought with them a new type of pottery drinking vessel known as a beaker; this earned them the soubriquet of the 'Beaker People'. They introduced metalworking and weaving and for the first time the people exhibited some concepts of social organisation and political power. Around 2000 BC carved designs on stone appeared of which the most common was the Cup and Ring mark. From 1500 BC to 500 BC farms were well established in the area which was warmer and drier than it is now. This process of human settlement culminated in the arrival of the Celtic-speaking peoples who hunted the well-established wild boars, deer, wolves and bears hereabouts.

The burial is the most significant monument left to us by

St Andrews' early inhabitants, and the 1975—77 excavations at Hallowhill, for instance, with its 140 known graves, along with earlier finds (1859—60) show the main early settlement areas. At first the early settlers cremated their dead and placed the ashes with grave goods in round or square cists. Between the fifth to ninth centuries the long cist was the most popular type of burial. In this type the body was laid full-length in the graves wherein the sides, roof and floor were made of slabs. From the discoveries we can see that St Andrews' headland was an early settlement area, probably as far as the end of modern Market Street; on the site of Dr Mudie's house in Market Street cinerary urns were found in 1867, and another at the junction of Church Street and Market Street in 1864. The early settlers also colonised the banks of the Kinness Burn, for urns have been found at Lawhead, and when ground was being levelled at Colonel Boothby's property at Balnacarron in 1859 and 1907 more burial urns were discovered. Settlements were also to be found, surrounded by the swamp forests of oak, pine and beach, at Dunork, Dunino and Drumcarrow.

When the Romans came Fife was the land of the Venicones, one of the tribes of the warrior society of Celtic peoples; and probably the first Roman soldiers to enter East Fife came as a consequence of Gnaeus Julius Agricola's movement northeast in 82 AD, although the Roman *exploratores* (the reconnaissance units of several kinds) may have done a survey by 79 AD. By the Flavian period of the late 80s AD, the neck of Fife from Forth to Tay was ringed with a line of forts from Camelon on the Antonine Wall, through Ardoch and Strageath to Bertha.

Archaeology shows that the largely philo-Roman Venicones, who fished St Andrews Bay and tilled the nearby hillsides, were a distinct cultural grouping, and probably enjoyed some protection from Rome. During 208—11 the Maeatae of central Scotland and the Caledonians of the north were in open revolt with Rome; the Maeatae occupied Fife and during the expedition against them of Emperor

Septimus Severus the only known Roman fort of consequence near to St Andrews was the thirty acre half-legion establishment built at Carpow for the II and VI Legions, on the south side of the Tay at Newburgh, near to where the Venicones had their fortress on Clatchard Craig. Carpow fort was evacuated and demolished a short time after Severus's death in 211. Carpow too, which was probably the *Orrea* mentioned by the geographer Ptolemy, may have been the northern end of a Roman road which crossed the marshlands of central Fife from Queensferry to the Tay.

Three other Roman forts lie in a line showing the Roman penetration of Fife down the River Eden; there is the 63-acre marching-camp at Auchtermuchty; the encampment at Edenwood, Cupar; and the nearest to St Andrews is the 35-acre site at Bonnytown near the junction of the Cameron and Kinaldy burns, west of Boarhills. All of these were temporary camps and may have been used only by the *exploratores*, but we do not know for sure exactly why the Romans came. As Fife was probably important to the Romans as a local source of coal, salt and grain, modern excavation and research does not rule out the possibility of a Roman camp of some kind (although now totally obliterated) on the site of modern St Andrews; in 1979 a worn Roman coin (an *antoninianus* of M. Piavonius Victorinus) of *circa* 268 was found in the grounds of St Leonards School, and may have been in use at a native site of that period in St Andrews. By 297 the foremost of Rome's chief enemies in Scotland, the *Picti* (the painted men) had become a powerful grouping and the power of Rome declined.

Most of our early information about the Picts comes from the Romans, but they do not come fully into historical focus until they were written about by the Venerable Bede (*circa* 673−735) in his *History*, which he completed in 731. Bede divided the Picts into two territorial groupings, the northern and southern, of whose realm the latter included the area of modern St Andrews. Tradition puts St Andrews within *Fib* (from which we get Fife), one of the four provinces of the southern Picts. Pictish St Andrews lasted until around 850.

Christianity first came to the land of the Picts around 565, when the abbot and confessor St Columba and his followers ventured from Ireland and settled in Iona. The Picts now followed the rule of the Celtic church of Columba and were often at war with their southern neighbours the Northumbrians. By 634 Northumbria was evangelised by Celtic monks from Iona, invited to the wild, windswept eastern coastlands by the Northumbrian king. Here they met the opposition of the Roman church which had been proselytised by St Augustine's Roman mission and at the Synod of Whitby. During 663−4 the Roman church prevailed and the Celtic church retreated to the west whence it came. In 710, Nechtan, convert King of the Picts, took up the ritual of the Roman church, having sought the advice of the abbot of St Peter's at Monkwearmouth, Northumbria, and by 717 he had expelled the Celtic monks from his kingdom. There were fundamental differences between the Celtic church and that of Rome — such as the date of Easter and the use of the tonsure by clerics — but the new rule of Rome was utilised in St Andrews and hence there came the link between St Andrews and the Northumbrian architects.

When the Columban communities decayed, their place was taken by the Celtic speaking Culdees, who nominally conformed to Rome. The Culdees — from *céli dé* 'companions of God' — were a loose assemblage of non-celibate individuals, whose earliest occurrences on record come from the first half of the ninth century. The Culdees patterned their life on such desert hermits as those of Syria and dwelt in *carcairs* (houses like boxes of stone) set around their church of timber and turf. These contemplative anchorites ceased to be hermits by the ninth century and evolved as an organised community and by 921 they were a canonical body of thirteen persons. A church was built for the Culdees at St Andrews before 877 by Constantine II and Constantine III became abbot of the Culdees and died among them at Kirkhill in 952. Tradition has it that their first church was set on Lady's Craig Rock, at the end of the present pier, but tide and storm forced the clerics to build a new church on the rocky headland above. That church was to develop into that of the Blessed Mary of the Rock, the ruins of which can still be seen at Kirkhill where they were discovered in 1860; the exposed nave is twelfth century and the choir is thirteenth century, and the footings of the altar and sedilla remain.

The Culdees had a distinct presence in the early medieval burgh. William Reeves, Bishop of Down, an acknowledged Culdee scholar, writing in 1860, tells us that by 1144 there were two bodies of clergy in St Andrews, the Culdees and the Canons Regular who came to form the chapter of the cathedral. But the Culdees, as a basic conservative Celtic body, were to survive the provisions of king, pope and bishop, even though the intention was for the Culdees to be absorbed into the cathedral chapter. Indeed it was not until 1273 that the Culdees were barred from their right to take part in the election of a bishop. The Culdee clergy — who became less and less Celtic — were presided over by a Provost and became a collegiate church, *Collegium Sanctae Mariae Virginis in Rupe*, one of the earliest in Scotland and by the thirteenth century they were a Chapel Royal. The chapel lost its royal dignity by the end of the fifteenth century, which honour passed in James III's day to Restalrig, near Edinburgh, and to Stirling in the reign of James IV.

The Culdees survived excommunication and many disputes with the later priory and continued to be mentioned in the records of St Andrews until 1332. Some Culdees rose to very high office; acting-Provost Adam de Makerston was one, a royal negotiator and representative of the Bishop of St Andrews in 1259 and a papal chaplain; William Wishart, who became archdeacon of St Andrews, Chancellor of the kingdom and Bishop of St Andrews in 1272, was another prominent Culdee. So by the thirteenth century the Culdees had developed from a Celtic clergy to a prominent secular body of important negotiators and by 1309 they still held their possessions in the *Cursus Apri*; their lands had included Kinkell, Lambieletham and Kingask. Although the position of the Culdees was impaired after the fourteenth century their collegiate church remained in St Andrews until the Reformation. John Leslie, Bishop of Ross, tells us that in June 1559 the Earl of Argyll and the Prior of St Andrews, afterwards the Earl of Moray, pulled down the church.

CHAPTER 2

Out of a Saint's Misfortune

The first date we can be sure about concerning St Andrews is 746, the year the usually reliable eleventh century monk Tigernach of Clonmacnoise records as the death of Tuathalan, Abbot of Cennrigmonaid, Gaelic for 'The Head of the King's mount': *Mors Tuathalain abbatis Cinrighmonai* wrote Tigernach. Cennrigmonaid was to be the first known name of the place that is now St Andrews and in the twelfth century this became the Latin Kilrimont when *Kil* (church) replaced *Kin* (headland). At this point we have the scenario for the substantial development of the religious site of St Andrews.

How St Andrew, the brother of Simon Peter and disciple of St John the Baptist, came to be associated with Cennrigmonaid is a confusing story of which there are two main legends. Both of these legends were written after the Augustinian canons established themselves there in the twelfth century. Version one, of *circa* 1165, tells us how King Angus I (731—61), son of Fergus, was raiding in the Merse (modern Berwickshire), when he came across a hostile enemy from the south of the Tweed. Walking with his earls, Angus witnessed a flash of blinding light and heard the voice of St Andrew, Christ's first disciple, calling Angus to face the enemy bearing before his army the Cross of Christ. This, it appears, Angus did and won his battle. Meanwhile, continued the monkish chronicler, an angel was guiding from Constantinople, capital of the Eastern Roman Empire, one of the guardians of the corpse of the Apostle to the safe anchorage at the summit of the king's hill 'that is *Rigmund*' (the name survives in the two farms of Easter and Wester Balrymonth — 'village of the king's hill' — to the south of

9

the town). The guardian was the monk called St Rule, or St Regulus, who met Angus at the gate of the king's encampment, probably on the site of the later castle. To further celebrate his victory over his enemies, Angus pledged the whole thirty acre site of Cennrigmonaid to the Glory of God and to St Andrew. It is related too, that, led by St Rule bearing the holy relics of the Apostle on his head, his chanting companions and the king and his earls made a circuit of Kirkhill whereon they erected twelve consecrated crosses to mark out the holy ground.

The second version of *circa* 1279 also cites St Rule and makes him a bishop, bringing him from Patras in Achaia, Greece, where St Andrew had been martyred on the distinctive cross called a *crux decussata* which has entered Scottish heraldry as the patriotic Saltire. St Andrew was martyred some time during the reign of Emperor L. Domitius Claudius Nero and because the Emperor Constantine was bent on taking the cadaver of St Andrew to Constantinople, Bishop Rule was commanded by an angel to extract a tooth, a kneecap, an upper arm-bone and three fingers of the saint's right hand and secrete them for further use.

Meanwhile, Angus the High King was encamped near the mouth of the Tyne to fight Athelstan, King of the West Saxons. Before the pitched battle Angus had a vision of St Andrew who subsequently gave him victory over superior odds. The angel who had commanded Rule to secure the relics of Andrew, now sent him to 'the utmost part of the world' with the relics. Thus, Rule and his companions set off with their sacred trust and journeyed west for eighteen months, landing in the midst of a storm at the place called Muckross, 'the headland of the boars, soon to be called Kilrimont. Rule and his followers waded ashore and erected a cross to defy the demons of the place. In due course Rule met Angus who endowed the bishop with land and twelve crosses were set up at Kilrimont round a dedicated precinct that was the new home for Andrew's bones. Indeed the holy

The noble Romanesque mid-11th century tower and choir of the Church of St Regulus, or St Rule, soars 108ft above the cathedral cemetery. The church was the precursor of its neighbour the Cathedral and was the first church of the Augustinian Priory of St Andrews. According to legend the relics of St Andrew, brought to the site by the Greek monk St Regulus, once lay in this church.

men built seven churches at Kilrimont; one to St Rule their leader; St Aneglas the Deacon; St Michael the Leader of the Heavenly Host (for it is said that Rule stepped ashore on 29 September the 'Night of St Michael'); also to the Blessed Virgin; St Damian the Martyr; St Bridget, founder of the Abbey of Kildare; and one to the Virgin Muren, daughter of Queen Finchem. All of these churches would be small wattle and daub buildings and the place thereafter was established as an area for pilgrimages.

Those interested in the foundation story of St Andrews may like to know that in *A History of Northumberland* (1896), in discussing the history of the church and priory of St Andrew at Hexham which was built by St Wilfred, Archbishop of York (634—709), there is a reference to one Prior Richard of Hexham who tells the story of Wilfred's successor, Acca, as bishop of the see.

Acca was driven from his bishopric in 733 and is purported to have removed some 'relics' of St Andrew. Indeed if any such relics were removed they are likely to have been *brandea* — pieces from garments — as any corporeal relics would have been considered too precious to allow away from the abbey precincts. However, Richard asserted, and it is a story given credence by the historian William Forbes Skene (1807—92), author of *Celtic Scotland*, that Acca went northwards and founded St Andrews. This can be discounted as being unprovable, but it is possible that the High King Angus acquired relics of Andrew from Acca. In historic reality, of course, there is no authentic account of the removal of St Andrew's bones from Constantinople.

Scholars have speculated as to who Rule was, and in his book on St Andrews the Greek Classicist, the late Professor Douglas Young (1913—73), averred that he was possibly the first Bishop of Senlis in the French *département* of Oise, who was born in fourth century Greece and was called St Rieul by the French. The tower in the cathedral precinct called St Rule's, or St Regulus', was not called by these names until around the year 1500.

St Rule's Cave, abutting the East Scores, was long pointed out as a holy place, but it is certainly an eighteenth century romantic invention latched onto by Sir Walter Scott (who loved such tushery about hermits) for mention in *Marmion* ('The Castle', Canto I, v. 29.):

> To fair St Andrews bound,
> Within the ocean-cave to pray,
> Where good Saint Rule his holy lay,
> From midnight to the dawn of day,
> Sung to the billow's sound.

There is more than just a hint, of course, that Rule was entirely fictitious, the invention of monkish hands. These medieval stories, then, about Acca, Angus and Rule, were part of the religious propaganda of the time to establish St Andrews as a site which predated Canterbury, Iona and Whithorn.

An important part of the traditional land endowment of the monastery which developed at Kilrimont was the *Cursus Apri Regalis*, the run of the royal wild boar. This parcel of land ran from present St Andrews to modern Boarhills, then westwards to include Cameron and Kemback and the land south of the Eden to within a mile or two of Cupar. When Alexander I regranted the *Cursus Apri Regalis* in the twelfth century he presented to the then monastery a set of 16 inch boar's tusks, which were fixed by silver chains to the altar of St Andrew. Thus was a Pictish fetish firmly placed within the relics of the monastery. In time the arms of the burgh of St Andrews reflected these factors. The extant arms of the burgh are a rearrangement of the device on the reverse of an old burgh seal of 1357 and are described thus in the *Lyon Register* (1912): 'Parted per pale Azure and Argent: in the dexter, on a mount in base the figure of Saint Andrew Proper, bearing his cross in front of him Argent; in the sinister, growing out of a mount in base an oak tree Proper, fructed Or, in front of the trunk of a boar passant Sable, langued Gules, armed Or.' Above the shield is set 'a mural crown and in an Escrol below the shield' the modern motto *Dum Spiro Spero* ('While I breathe, I hope'). Writing in his *Cosmography*, the ecclesiastical writer Peter Heylyn (1600–62) tells how King Angus established 'The Order of St Andrew' as the 'principal order of knighthood' in the kingdom. Heylyn says: 'The knights did wear about their necks a Collar laced with Thistles, with the picture of St Andrew appendant to it; the motto *Nemo me impune lacessit* ('No one provokes me with impunity') — the motto and precursor of The Most Ancient and Most Noble Order of the Thistle founded in 1687.

In 906 St Andrews became the seat of the Bishop of Alba and by 975 the diocese of St Andrews was expanded by the inclusion of lands from Forth to Tweed wherein the Bishop of St Andrews was *primus inter pares* (the senior bishop amongst equals): indeed the alternative title of the Bishop of St Andrews until the thirteenth century was *episcopus Scottorum*. The first name we have for a bishop of St Andrews is Cellach during the reign of Constantine II (903–43) of the dynasty of MacAlpin and Dunkeld/Canmore, who retired to the abbey-church (maybe only his personal cell within the grouping of seven small churches) at Kirkhill. It is said that the fifth known early bishop, Cellach II (971–96), son of Ferdlag, was the first Scottish bishop to travel to Rome to have his episcopate confirmed.

During the episcopate of Fothad II (1059–93) two important events happened which were to change the whole aspect of the holy enclave of Kilrimont; first, there was the coming of the Normans, and, secondly, a new church was built probably near the site of an older church; this new church is known to us today as St Rule's or St Regulus' (Tower). In medieval records this church is called 'the old church', but the Dundee-born historian Hector Boece (*circa* 1465–1536) referred to it as *diui Reguli templum*, the Church of St Rule, from which its modern name derives.

Norman rule came to Scotland peacefully when Malcolm III (1058–93) surrendered to William the Conqueror within

The fine pre-Norman features of the Northumbrian school of architecture at St Regulus Church still show the raggle marks of the subsequent roofs which covered the choir and nave. Major alterations were made to the building when plans were being considered by Bishop Robert during 1124—44, to install the community of Augustinian canons here (*Peter Adamson*).

the shadow of the round tower at Abernethy in 1072. By this time Malcolm had married for his second wife, Margaret granddaughter of Edmund Ironside. Margaret had fled to Scotland with her sister Christina and brother Edgar Atheling, as refugees of the Norman invasion. A devoted churchwoman, Margaret set about introducing more refined fashions to the Scottish court and with her husband's acquiescence enthusiastically overhauled religious practice in Scotland, instituting the use of the Roman rite, clerical celibacy, the keeping of Lent, the Easter mass and the observance of Sunday, amongst other things. From the works of her confessor and biographer, Turgot, Prior of Durham, we learn that she patronised Scotland's existing religious houses. By the twelfth century, incidentally, Fife is being described as a 'region' governed firmly by a sub-king as the Kingdom of Fife.

Margaret corresponded with Lanfranc, Archbishop of Canterbury, and brought Benedictine monks to Dunfermline to found the famous abbey. Importantly for St Andrews she is believed to have persuaded Malcolm to concede the ecclesiastical overlordship of the Archbishop of York, and Bishop Fothad II professed submission to the archbishop. Thus the Scottish church was given over to Norman bishops and Fothad was the last of what might be called the Celtic bishops of St Andrews. Margaret was the catalyst that gave modern St Andrews its birth and the Normans brought their own clergy, a thorough ecclesiastical reorganisation and monastic settlement. By 1107 Turgot became the first Norman bishop of St Andrews and until 1238 the see was the largest and wealthiest in Scotland, containing the most important burghs in the kingdom, and governed by a very remarkable succession of Norman bishops.

A further look at St Rule's Tower gives the next important stepping stone to the St Andrews story. The first church of St Rule can be dated to the 1070s and was intended basically as a 'reliquary' church. It had a small chapel (26' x 20') and a fourteen and a half foot square tower rising to one hundred and eight feet; it became a wonderful landmark to guide pilgrims to the heart of the cult of Scotland's patron saint. Within the chapel, and probably set upon its main altar, would be the relics of the Apostle. As we shall see, this church was greatly altered by Bishop Robert who set in motion the ecclesiastical site that we know as St Andrews today.

CHAPTER 3

The Wonder of Christendom

Eadmer of Canterbury, who wrote a contemporary Latin chronicle down to 1122 called *Historia Novorum in Anglia*, had succeeded Turgot as Bishop of St Andrews after a five year interregnum 1115–20 in which the affairs of St Andrews had been administered by William a monk of Bury St Edmunds on behalf of the king. But, Eadmer's rule was so undermined by Alexander I that he returned to Canterbury to be replaced by the Anglo-Norman prior Robert. When Robert came to St Andrews, St Rule's church was deemed inadequate for the development of the new ecclesiastical plans for the site. Robert, who was then still prior of the Augustinian abbey of Scone, had been nominated bishop by Alexander I before 1124 and he was consecrated by Thurston, Archbishop of York in 1127, by which time Robert was resident at Kilrimont. St Rule's church was to be the cathedral of Robert's see and to act as a priory church for a new ecclesiastical order which was to dwell in its shadow. The church was extended to include a nave of some sixty feet by twenty seven feet and its new form took in a central tower, nave, choir and sanctuary with a total length of one hundred and twenty five feet. It is probably the work of a Yorkshire mason from Nostell Priory, West Yorkshire, brought by Bishop Robert. On the eastern face of the tower can be seen the three raggles of the roof — the centre one is probably marking the height of the original roof. It is thought that the top raggle is that of a thirteenth century roof and the bottom one of the roof built by Prior William de Lothian (1340–54). The south doorway and the staircase is considered to have been built in the sixteenth century. At the east end of the remaining choir is the plaque reading: 'THIS WAS REPAIRED AT THE EXPENSE OF THE EXCHEQUER 1780 BY R. THOMPSON'.

The parishioners of Kilrimont, and of Robert's new 'burgh of St Andrew', were now served by a church dedicated to the Holy Trinity just a little to the north west of St Rule's church, perhaps on the site of one of the defunct Celtic chapels. While the work was being undertaken for the new church the clergy would probably live in timber conventual buildings around St Rule's.

Today the ecclesiastical site which visitors see includes St Rule's Tower, the ruined cathedral and the equally ruined priory and their associated buildings. As the cathedral was administered by the priory and had its birth amongst the canons who were to care for it, it is perhaps best that we begin an examination of the site from the priory.

Although the cathedral was the central building of an important diocese it did not stand alone, for immediately to the south of its nave stood the cloister and conventual buildings of the Priory of the Augustinian Canons which had been established by Bishop Robert. The first Augustinian house in Scotland was the one founded by Alexander I, around 1120, at Scone, and colonised by six clergy from the priory of St Oswald at Nostell. Bishop Robert's priory at St Andrews was founded and endowed by 1144 and he gave to it, by this year, such lands as those of Strathkinness. Prior Robert of St Oswald's, Nostell, was its first prior and soon after its foundation David I visited the site. The priory rapidly grew in influence; in 1147 Pope Eugenius III gave the rights of electing the bishop of the see to the priory and its clergy instead of the Culdees, for it had been Bishop Robert's resolve to eject the Culdees from the ancient site as they were secular and married men who could not (and would not) conform with sincerity to the self-denying ordinances of his Augustinian clergy.

The clergy at St Andrews priory followed the Rule of St Augustine (354—430), Bishop of Hippo, a Roman from the province of Numidia (modern Algeria) who served as Public Orator at Milan. He was baptised by St Ambrose, Bishop of Milan, into Catholic Christianity, and became an intellectual genius who was to dominate Latin theology for centuries. In 388 he established a monastic-like community at his family home at Thagaste and pursued his own 'theology', a blend of Biblical study and contemplation, interlarded with religious argument. His great works are his *Confessions* and *The City of God.* Augustine's Rule survived the occupation of the barbarians and towards the end of the eleventh century communities of canons regular began to evolve. What made them different from cloistered monks was that they observed more freedom for active work in the community than was set down in the more common Rule of St Benedict. So the canons of St Andrews were more worldly than monks, and left their cloisters to minister to the people in parish churches and carry out the church business. Of the Augustinians the thirteenth century musician-turned-monk Guyot de Provins says: 'Augustine's Rule is more courteous than Benedict's. Among them, one is well shod, well clothed, well fed. They go out when they like, mix with the world, and talk at table.' By 1418 the prior of St Andrews enjoyed the use of the *pontificalia* — the wearing of a mitre — and James V described the priory in his *Letters* as 'the first and most famous monastic house in Scotland'.

The ruins as seen today are scraps of the work of Prior John White, and of his successor John de Haddington and are of the period 1236—58. They were improved by Prior William de Lothian around the middle of the fourteenth century. The buildings of the priory were set around the square made by the cloister which itself was linked to the church by east and west processional doorways. So located to secure the maximum sunshine, the cloister was a place of tranquillity and seclusion from daily life and as a rule conversation was forbidden within its walls. Here walks might be taken and literary study indulged. The cloister had four covered walkways with roofs supported by open arches which would probably be glazed by the fifteenth century. The cloister garth in the centre was sown with grass. The cloister too would probably be used as a schoolroom for the novices and as a *scriptorium*; book recesses can still be seen in the north-eastern part of the cloister. On the floor straw, hay or mats would be strewn for warmth and quietness.

Abutting the south transept gable lay the east range of the priory, divided from the gable by a slype (passage) leading to the priory cemetery and probably the now vanished infirmary and misericord; the slype also acted as an inner parlour (or, talking place) and had a bench along its wall; its gutter still remains. The main building in the two-storey east range was the chapter house with its doorway dating from 1160-*circa* 1200; this building was extended eastwards during 1313–21 at the expense of Bishop Lamberton and Prior John of Forfar, and the stone benches where the clergy sat to discuss everyday affairs can still be seen. The floor of the chapter house was used as a burial area for the senior clergy and stone coffins may still be examined *in situ.*

The chief use of the priory chapter house was for the meetings of all the canons, ranged in order of seniority, the youngest nearest the door. A chapter meeting was held weekly at which commemorations of benefactors, past priors and martyrs took place and *obits* and a *requiescant in pace.* It was a place of business and news, and discipline was administered to any erring canons after a confession of fault or an accusation. Punishment was meted out for 'light faults' such as separation from the common table, or a lower place in the chapter or choir and reduction of food. For grave faults, the greatest humiliation was prostration at the church door where every canon going into the choir would step over the culprit's body. Corporal punishment was not unknown.

Next to the chapter house is a chamber which was probably used as a vestry and maybe the prior's lodging before a separate house was built to the east (where the museum for gravestones of post-Reformation period is now located). The south wall of this vestry was next to the day-stair which led up to the *dorter* (dormitory) which linked across the chapter house to the night-stair into the south transept of the cathedral. Hay was put on the floor of the *dorter* and beds were of straw; probably the sub-priors had beds of oak near the door, but all had no more than a mat by the bed, a woollen covering, and a woollen cloth under a hard pillow. Beyond the day-stair is the *calefactorium* (warming house) with its access doors to the cloister and the *necessarium* (latrine) which would probably be linked by a covered way. The warming house contained the only fireplace common to the community. The *Cloacina Maxima* (great drain) of the *necessarium*, also called the *rere-dorter*, can still be seen to the south of the site.

Within the south range of the cloister only the sub-croft remains, above which was the *frater* or *refectorium* (dining hall) and this was reconstructed at the end of the nineteenth century. Herein would be a high table, probably on a dais, where sat the senior clergy and perhaps important guests. There was no fireplace in the *frater*, but maybe a brazier was allowed in winter. At the beginning of the meal a *skilla*, or gong, would be struck and a grace said by the precentor. During the meals the canons would be read to from a pulpit.

The western range of the cloister is only represented today by the barrel-vaulted cellars on the site of the Senzie (Synod) House. This house was used as a council-hall after the Reformation but during the time of the canons it became the sub-prior's residence. It gave its name to the medieval Senzie Fair. Within the cloister garth was held the Senzie Fair for a fortnight after Easter. Scots, Flemings, Frenchmen and Englishmen all came to buy wools, skins, salmon and beasts, and sell linen, silk, tapestries, carpets, spices, wine, olive oil, armour, gold and silver ware and cutlery. Under the Senzie House may have been the *cellarium*, or place for stores. A mansion house was constructed above in the nineteenth century and the cloister was used as a garden, with greenhouses set against the south wall of the nave. The cloister was served by two deep wells and the one within the south cloister walk was the well of the *lavatorium*, where the clergy washed before entering the *frater*; nearby would be a cupboard of oak for clean towels.

St Andrews Augustinian priory had a dual function; it was the home of the community of Canons Regular of the Order of St Augustine and it was the administration centre of the Cathedral Chapter of the Diocese. By and large the Bishop/Archbishop was their superior and chose their Prior (with their agreement), but in reality the canons conducted and controlled their own affairs. Within the cathedral it was the duty of the canons to supervise maintenance work on the fabric and conduct the services; as priests, rather than monks, the majority of the clerics would be ordained and would be expected to say Mass once a day at one of the many altars in the cathedral. From their number came the officers of the cathedral. The head of the chapter — an assembly of the canons of the cathedral — was the Prior, who also would act as Dean of the cathedral, and as Vicar-General when the Bishop was absent or unable to carry out his duties. There is evidence that clergy retired from other parts of the country would help the prior too; the diocesan bishop seems to have had a suffragan from time to time when the bishop was away on state affairs; we know that one such was Edward Stewart, Bishop of Orkney, who retired to St Andrews and that William Gibson, Bishop of Libaria, was suffragan to Cardinal Archbishop David Beaton. The prior's assistants were the sub-prior and the *tertius prior.*

The personnel of the priory and the cathedral had different areas for which they were responsible: the *sacristan* had charge of the church building, the holy vessels of the altar, the valuable linen, embroidered robes and the banners for the procession on saints' days, the *chamberlain* was responsible for the day to day clothes of the clerics as well as organising the four-times-a-year baths. The *sacristan* saw, too, that the church was clean and looked after the lighting — he probably employed a layman to keep the warning sea light lit on the precinct wall. His assistant, the *sub-sacristan,* saw to the ringing of the bells for services and to the supply of 'live-coals' in iron dishes to warm the hands in winter of the priests ministering at the altars. The *infirmarian* acted as physician, barber and keeper of the *herbarium* within the gardens to the south of the priory precinct where the St Leonard's girls' school playingfields are today. The *precentor*, or *armarius*, acted as librarian and the *almoner* dealt with succour for the needy. The *cellarer*, kitchener and *pittancer* looked after food supplies and cooking and the latter looked after the extra rations, 'pittances' on feast days and special occasions. The *refectorian* tended to the arrangements for serving meals and for the hygiene of the *lavatorium*. The *grainger* was in charge of the grain supplies for the *pistrinum* (bakehouse) and *bracium* (brewhouse) and the collection of 'teinds' (tithes) for the *granarium*.

It is known that St Andrews priory also had a *bedellus*, a messenger, a compiler of the breviaries and a canon skilled in calligraphy and miniature illumination. The university still retains the position of 'bedellus', an archbeadle who is the principal macebearer and executive agent of the university. Most of the canons would be craftsmen in their own right and some of them would be men of great academic distinction. One of the canons would also have charge of the novices coming into the order. There were probably no more than forty canons resident at the priory at any one time.

The canons' daily life was strictly regulated by time. Not long ago a fifteenth century manuscript was found in Italy which showed a clock locking plate for striking the Canonical Hours (*canonicae horae*). This manuscript was written by one Benvenuto di Lorenzo della Volpaia and gave vital clues as to how the clerics of such ecclesiastical foundations as St Andrews regulated the times of divine service. The Canonical Hours — the times of daily prayers — were laid down by the church breviaries which regulated the divine services appointed to be recited at these hours. Theologians believe that the seven hourly divisions of the day in the monastic world arose from *Psalm 119, v. 164* which in its medieval translation read: *Septies in die laudem dixi tibi* . . . ('Seven times in the day I have given praise to Thee'). It is known for

St Andrews Cathedral looking down the nave towards the east gable. Once the focal point of medieval St Andrews, the Cathedral was founded in 1160 by Arnold, Abbot of Kelso, and consecrated by Bishop William de Lamberton, in the presence of King Robert I, the Bruce, in 1318. The Cathedral had an original internal length of 357 feet, making it the largest church in Scotland, and the extant south wall shows that building began at the east end. The Cathedral was abandoned as a consequence of the Protestant Reformation in 1559.

sure that a timetable for prayer was established by the fifth century, for a regular cycle of prayer was first noted around 385 in *Peregrinatio Egeriae*, about a woman (Egeria) who visits Jerusalem. Some theology historians aver that the seven divisions of the monastic clock possibly began with the four Roman divisions of the day (*prima, tertia, sexta,* and *nona*) and the four night divisions of *vesper* (evening), *media nox* (midnight), *dilucesco* (cock's crow) and *aurora* (dawn). Further it is probable that St Benedict of Nursia, in his *Regula S. Benedicti* (Rule of St Benedict) was the first to give proper monastic place to the hours; but in the monasteries of Great

Britain these hourly divisions varied from winter to summer, and again they varied over the centuries. By and large the St Andrews canons' day was fourteen hours long. When the priory of St Andrews functioned at its height the canons would be regulated approximately thus:

2.00 am. Arise.	The sub-prior checked the time and rang the bell in the dormitory. Throughout the waking hours gongs would be struck in accord with the practice of *tabula sonatilla* — striking to remind the canons of their passage through the earthly state.
2.15/2.30 am.	Prayers; psalms. Soft 'night bell' would be rung in church. Each service was preceded by a bell.
	MATINS (first service of the day).
	LAUDS.
	Return to sleep.
Dawn.	PRIME.
	Great bell summons servants and laity to early Mass.
	Reading in the cloister.
8.00 am.	Wash; *mixtum* (light breakfast).
	TIERCE.
	Morrow Mass.
9.00 am.	Meeting in the chapter house.
	Work.
	Reading.
Noon.	SEXT.
	High Mass.
	NONE.
	Dine.
2.30 pm.	Reading.
	Work.
5.00 pm.	VESPERS.
	Supper.
6.00 pm.	COMPLINE (the last service of the day).
7.00 pm.	Retire.

The difficulty of calculating the hours before the invention of striking clocks is easy to appreciate. In the priory of St Andrews the mechanics for telling time had two main phases. First came the *gnomen*, the sun-clock, and the *solarium*, or sundial; secondly, were the sand-glasses, and the *clepsydrae*, the water-clocks. Not every monastery possessed any of these and some houses depended on such basic indications of time as cock-crow, the amount of wax consumed by the burning of a candle, or oil in a lamp, or by the movement of the stars. To help with the latter St Gregory of Tours wrote: *De cursu stellarum ratio, qualiter as officium implendum debeat observari,* ('The courses of the stars and how to observe them for the purpose of fulfilling the [*Divine*] Office'.)

At any one time two canons would be expected to keep watch on the passage of time by consulting the *horologium*, under the supervision of the sub-prior. By the sixteenth century the priory and cathedral would have had clocks gifted to them such as the monastic alarm clocks approved in fifteenth century Europe, bracket clocks, buttress clocks, pillar clocks and wisdom clocks, of which the latter were very popular in ecclesiastical circles. Known to French monks as *horloges de sapience*, these wisdom clocks had a 24-hour dial, were weight-driven and the dial revolved behind a fixed pointer. The symbolism of the clocks was founded on the *Book of the Wisdom of Solomon* and was a constant reminder of temperance; the controlled regulation of time was deemed a symbol of the great virtues of obedience, chastity, morality, duty, valour against evil and spiritual accomplishment. The disappearance of the priory and cathedral clocks is simply explained. Freestanding clocks were easy to purloin and sundials were fine additions to a laird's garden after the Reformation.

The liturgy used by the canons in the cathedral would be the *Sarum Rite* adapted for the metropolitan church, and the canonical hours would be interspersed when necessary with the special needs of the feast days, or the canons' individual masses, or such tasks as the blessing of the water at the altar

of Our Lady for the *asperges* (a short service introductory to
Mass) and the blessing of candles at Candlemass. The
cathedral also had a great musical tradition in which the
canons would be involved. Certainly there were St Andrews
composers like Patrick Hamilton who wrote a nine-part
Mass of St Michael, and Canon David Peebles (1530)
prepared a four-part arrangement of the Magnificat antiphon
for first Vespers of Whitsunday, the *Si quis diligit me*; thus the
priory sponsored a song school.

The Augustinian priory of St Andrews had three
dependant religious houses within its sway, Portmoak,
Pittenweem and Monymusk. Portmoak, sometimes called
Loch Leven Priory, had originally been a Culdee settlement,
and David I granted the island of Loch Leven to the
Augustinian canons around 1152, the same year that Bishop
Robert of St Andrews granted the priory of St Serf to the
same canons. The prior of the establishment probably acted
as the *tertius prior* of the priory at St Andrews. After the
Reformation the priory at Portmoak was granted to St
Leonard's College.

The priory at Pittenweem was founded before 1318 and
had a long and somewhat complicated history; beginning as
a Benedictine foundation on the Isle of May, it was formerly
the possession of the Abbey of Reading; throughout history
the designation of the priory was confusingly both 'May' and
'Pittenweem'. The priory was held *in commendam* by various
succeeding bishops and archbishops of St Andrews and in
1593 the priory property was granted to the magistrates and
community of the burgh of Pittenweem, and later it became
a temporal lordship for Frederick Stewart in 1606 with the
title of Lord Pittenweem (the peerage became dormant after
Stewart's death in 1625). The priory of Monymusk,
Aberdeenshire, founded by Gilchrist, Earl of Mar, before
1245, was also formerly a Culdee community, and its history
remains obscure; it was noted as being ruinous in 1550, and
records show that it was used as a quarry for the building of
the Forbes family castle at Monymusk.

The *circa* 1160–1200 east gable of St Andrews Cathedral, and the tower of St Regulus Church, seen over the retaining wall running along Gregory Place. When all of a piece the Cathedral consisted of a twelve-bay nave, north and south transepts, a central tower, and a six-bay choir with the shrine of the Apostle and Martyr Andrew at the east end (*Peter Adamson*).

The known subsidiary buildings of the priory were the Prior's House of 1403, the granary, demolished in 1655, the two Teinds Barns, the Abbey Mill, with brewhouse nearby, disused by 1861 and on the site of the sanatorium for St Leonard's School. The Royal Tennis Courts were located within the priory precincts, abutting the later gasometer of 1903. Undoubtedly a building of great importance within the precinct was the *Novum Hospitium*, or New Inns, which was later used as a royal residence by the Earl of Moray as Commendator and by James VI in 1580, and as the home of post-Reformation archbishops. It was sited near the 1894 hospice of St Leonard's School. The *Novum Hospitium* is believed to have been the last building erected in connection with the priory before the Reformation. The gateway to the *Novum Hospitium* of 1537 was restored in 1845 and 1894 and realigned down Pends Road as an entrance to the school Hospice. The gate bears the arms of Prior James Hepburn and the Royal Arms of Scotland. The priory guest house (*magna aula hospitium*) of *circa* 1350 was sited between the modern frontages of the buildings of St Leonard's School known as Bishopshall and St Rules; probably the guest house was on the site of a much earlier building; a portion of the wall and fireplace are to be seen within the boarding house quads.

The whole of the priory precinct was enclosed by a wall which remains the longest extent of early walling in Scotland, with a circuit that is almost complete. The wall we see today is of the early sixteenth century and is the work of the priorate of John Hepburn (who died in 1522), son of Patrick, Lord Hailes, whose heraldic panels proclaim him at different places as the builder. It is certain that Hepburn's walls were reconstructions of earlier walling, with the precinct known to have been enclosed from at least the fourteenth century: material of the older wall is still discernible at certain locations. The walls enclosed an area of around thirty acres and rise to twenty feet high and are three feet thick, and were fortified by attached round and square towers equipped with gun-loops, and embellished with canopied niches for sacred statues and heraldic panels. Only thirteen of the towers remain, but George Martine in his *Reliquiae Divi Andreae* (1797) recorded sixteen in 1683. By the sixteenth century, the cathedral itself was bounded by a now vanished spur of the precinct wall from the Pends gateway.

A circuit of the walls is easily made today and forms a delightful walk through history. It is good to start from the cathedral where Hepburn's walls begin at the late twelfth century east gable and where there is a gateway displaying the Hepburn arms (on a chevron, two lions combatant rending a rose, with pastoral staff behind and AD VITA [*M*] 'for life', from the old legal maxim referring to property conveyance *ad vitam aut culpam* 'for life or until a misdeed'). Next to the gateway is a round tower where a 'Turret Light' was fixed and where the 'White Light' was erected in 1849 serviced from the stair within.

The walls now run along the line of the cliffs, known hereabouts as 'Dane's Wark', to the so-called, gun-holed, 'Haunted Tower', which comprised a watch-room of sorts, a short stair and a vault below. After the Reformation, the tower room was appropriated as a mausoleum by such as the Martines, Lairds of Denbrae, which, when filled, was sealed. Two niches on the outside of the wall probably contained statues of the Blessed Virgin, one in her form of 'St Mary of the Rock' (in honour of the chapel on the cliff nearby) and the other with the infant Christ. In line with the niches is a panel with the Hepburn arms, surmounted by a pot of lilies to represent the beauty and purity of the Blessed Virgin.

The tower's upper room was opened in 1868 and a plethora of coffins and numerous bodies were uncovered. One, recounted Dr Hay Fleming, was 'a female, [who] had on her hands white leather gloves'. This cadaver was the basis of the story of the 'white lady' who is deemed to haunt this part of the old cathedral cemetery, and who fired Dean Linskill's over-heated imagination. The tower was again opened in

1888 when an iron grille was set in the long built-up doorway.

The next tower is round and is obscured on the inside by the sepulchral monument to the Playfair family. At this point the wall veers towards the harbour and at the actual turn a tower was removed, it seems, around 1880. The whole of this section of the wall was obscured by the Burgh Gasworks in 1835, and was only cleared in 1964. Here is to be found the round 'Inscription Tower' indicating that the wall was extended and adorned by John Hepburn's nephew, Patrick Hepburn, Bishop of Moray, one of the most immoral of the pre-Reformation prelates. The inscription on the tower reads: [*P*]RECESSORI[*S*] OP[*VS*] POR[*RO*]HIC PAT[*RICVS*] HEPBVRN EXCOLIT EGREBIVS ORBE SALVT [*IFERO*]: 'Here the excellent Patrick Hepburn in his turn embellishes the work of his predecessors with a tower of defence'.

Fronting the Inner Harbour and the East Bents stands the Mill Port, known in pre-Reformation times as the Sea Yett. It once had flanking towers and openings for the pouring of pitch on enemies assailing the gateway; here too were the Hepburn arms. To the right of the gateway's front stood the Shore Mill of *circa* 1518 (reconstructed in the seventeenth century and renovated 1964−66) a few yards away from the outlet of the *Cloacina Maxima.* A series of blocked-up doors and windows can still be seen along the shore wall from the Mill Port; it is likely that they served offices set behind the wall as the canons had seaborne goods to administer and store and probably fish taxes to collect.

At the end of the Shore road the Doocot Tower stands at an angle and it probably had a conical roof and pigeon holes. The triangle of land by the Doocot Tower marks the site of the East Toll House, which was demolished in 1933; Abbey Cottage of *circa* 1815 abuts the wall, but it had to be rebuilt after the fire of 1914. The gateway encountered up Abbey Walk is the Teinds Yett of 1516−30, which stood next to the great Teinds Barn; the gateway has a large aperture for waggons and a smaller one for pedestrians. This was the grand exit and entry to the south through which came the waggons with the 'teynd sheaves' at harvest time. The teinds, of course, were the Scottish equivalent of the English tithes due to the church. Marie de Guise-Lorraine entered the priory precincts in 1538 through this gateway on her way to her marriage with James V in the cathedral.

The Hepburn arms are to be seen in three places along the Abbey Wall section of the wall whose lower courses date from *circa* 1350 and its upper section is contemporary with the Teinds Yett. Probably there was a tower opposite the old burgh school and the remaining tower (opposite St Nicholas's residence, St Leonard's School) marked where the old priory wall swung sharply north to join with the gateway near St Leonard's chapel that bears the Lennox arms. The remainder of the wall (St Leonard's Wall) is much later than Prior Hepburn's work.

The gateway of the priory, colloquially called 'The Pends', is set at the end of South Street and linked up with the precinct walls. Today only the outer shell of the gateway remains with its wall springers to show where the upper floor began; the roadway is at a higher level than the medieval way through. The Pends dates from *circa* 1350 and its central arch was removed 1837—38. The Pends road probably followed an old track and was the main entrance into the domestic range of the priory; it was not opened as a public right of way until the nineteenth century. Some sixty seven feet by twenty one feet, the gateway had a porter's room by the great wooden entrance door and a side entrance where visitors would make enquiries is still in place.

Outwith the precincts, and at a distance of about one mile near to the sea (where the current swimming pool complex of 1988 now stands and the old site of St Nicholas farm) stood a foundation connected with the priory. The lazar, or leper Hospital of the Blessed Nicholas of St Andrews was probably founded by the Prior and Canons of St Andrews and is one of the earliest leper hospitals in Scotland. In those days the term leprosy described any disease from lupus (tuberculosis of the skin) to erysipelas (St Anthony's Fire). Between 1188 and 1202, Bishop Roger de Beaumont gave to the hospital the lands of Peekie (then Putekin) and William the Lion confirmed the hospital's charters and gave the administrators a team of horses to bring their own brushwood from Kingsmuir (Crail). The lepers were allowed to beg at their own gate on the St Andrews-Crail road, and the Third Lateran Council allowed for lepers to have their separate places of worship. Thus the enclave at St Nicholas would probably have living quarters, a chapel, a churchyard and its own clergy. As the disease began to die out, the inmates at St Nicholas would dwindle and as it was described in 1438 as 'a poor's hospital' it may have just become a place of sanctuary for the infirm poor. The later uses of the buildings are obscure, but its endowments, revenues and clergy were absorbed by the Dominican Friars at their house in South Street by 1529 and it remained some kind of poorhouse until 1583.

Probably before he died in 1153, Bishop Robert had planned a great new cathedral, but the actual foundation of the cathedral we know today was not undertaken until the time of his successor, Bishop Arnold in 1160. By this time too the old designation of Kilrimont was being replaced by the name of the Apostle to identify bishopric, burgh, precinct and church. As with the priory, the cathedral church of St Andrews had a dual purpose; it was the cathedral church of the diocese of St Andrews and it was the church of the Augustinian Canons. Until modern times it was the largest edifice ever built in Scotland and probably contained the largest collection of medieval art ever gathered together in Scotland.

The relic cathedral we see today is the work of many centuries and in its first form it ran to over 320ft long and 168ft across its transepts which formed the crosspiece of its cruciform shape. In time it was to exceed 391 ft in length and have fourteen bays, making it the longest church in Britain save that at Norwich. Its length today is 357 ft. We can get some idea of the height for the extant south nave wall — a mixture of architecture from 1160—1279 — rises to its full original height. The cathedral was begun in 1160 by Bishop Robert's successor, Arnold, Abbot of the Tironensian monastery at Kelso with the active encouragement of Malcolm IV. Arnold had been consecrated in the church of St Rule in 1159 by William, Bishop of Moray, the Pope's legate. Building began at the east end and the outer walls of the choir, the transepts and ten nave bays would be completed in one building phase. The stone probably came from the Strathkinness area, but the masons used stonework culled from the Celtic sites around as seen in identified fragments in the east gable (the only major twelfth century gable to survive in Scotland). Phase one of the work was completed around 1190. Bishop Arnold died in 1163 and was buried, as Bishop Robert had been, in St Rule's church, but the building went on; indeed eleven successive prelates continued the work, and although they had a direct hand in keeping the work going the actual administration and construction decisions were carried out by the canon-appointed sacrist — he was also known as 'master of the fabric'. The building would be usable as a cathedral and priory church around 1230 and we know that in 1238 Bishop Malvoisine, the last of the Anglo-Norman bishops, was buried in the south aisle of the choir which had been constructed during his own episcopate.

We know little or nothing of the masons themselves who worked on the fabric, but the extant records recall the *custos fabricae*, the *custos operum* and the *magister operacionum* who toiled on the work along with the hundreds of suppliers of material, the quarry-workers, masons, lime burners, mortar mixers, joiners, iron workers, timber scaffolders, crane operators, plankers, template-makers, carters, and hewers. But in the west wall of the south transept of St Mary's Cistercian abbey at Melrose there is a plaque set as a posthumous testimonial to a master-mason who worked on St Andrews cathedral:

> John Morrow sum tym callit was I,
> And born in Parysse certanly,
> And had in kepyng and mason werk
> Of santandroys ye hye kirk
> Of Glasgo, Melros, and Paslay
> Of Nyddysdayll and of Galway
> I pray to God, Mari bathe
> & swete Sanct Johne, to kepe
> This haly kirk fra skathe.

Work on the cathedral construction continued at a steady rate and by the episcopate of Bishop William Wishart (1271−79) the cathedral was well on towards its conclusion. Hardly had the west gable been completed than it was blown down in a gale. It was decided to rebuild the new gable two bays shorter than the old one, thus reducing the nave by thirty four feet, and this allowed room for a *narthex* (a porch) also called a Galilee for the great west door, an unusual innovation in Scotland. The whole building was now available for use and consisted of a nave, the choir with its wooden seats for the clergy and the sanctuary under the great east window. The north and south transepts shared the choir. The nave, incidentally, would be empty of seats, the pilgrims or parishioners kneeling or standing, but along its north and south walls would be low stone seats for the infirm to rest − from these seats we have our proverb 'the weakest go to the wall'. In Prior James Haldenstone's day, as we shall see, the nave itself contained eighteen of the cathedral's thirty one altars, but in its earliest form it would be empty. The nave ended at the choir screen.

The north aisle of the nave, called the Archdeacon's Aisle, had a small projection called the Consistory House, where administrative discussions took place, probably with an altar

to St John the Evangelist by its door. At the northwest corner
of the nave stood the chapel of St John the Baptist with the
baptismal font nearby; and in the southwest corner, the
aspersorium, the holy water stoup into which the pilgrims
dipped their fingers to cross themselves. At the east end of
the nave the cathedral well may still be found, out of which
water was drawn for the liturgical ceremonies, for washing
and so on; it was probably first used as a source of water for
the building of the cathedral. In medieval times the well
probably had an ornate cover. It is likely too that there
would be a clock of some kind in the nave, and succeeding
bishops and priors added to the furniture of the whole
cathedral.

The choir, of prime import amongst the holy areas of the
cathedral, was located at the east end of the church in front
of the high altar. Two aisles divided the choir stalls from the
outer walls and herein were the tombs of bishops Trail,
Lamberton, Gamelin, Malvoisine, de Gullane and Wishart.
To the right and left of the choir door probably stood altars
to the saints Peter and Paul. Above the western entrance to
the choir stood the Holy Rood (the Cross of Christ Crucified),
a gift of Saint Margaret, set on its beam and flanked by
figures of the Blessed Virgin and St John, representing the
attendant church. The Rood Loft was where the Gospel was
read at Mass and sometimes for the Altar of the Rood where
the Rood Light was the most important after the Sanctuary
Light (indicating Christ's presence in the tabernacle). The
choir also contained the choir lectern in the centre and the
bishop/archbishop's chair. In front of the entrance to the
choir was the huge choir screen to protect the sacred areas.
The floor of the choir was paved with large tiles of black and
brown, and yellow and green, laid diagonally; most of these
were made locally at the priory kiln and the more ornate
were probably imported from the Low Countries. A set of
tiles has been reconstructed *in situ* in the north part of the
choir. Besides the choir, tiled areas of the east end would
include the altar to the Blessed Virgin, in the north aisle,

The 30-acre cathedral and priory precinct was surrounded by a wall 20ft in height, over half a mile long, and 3ft thick. The wall was reconstructed by Prior John Hepburn (d.1522) and his successor and nephew, Prior Patrick Hepburn, Bishop of Moray. Fortified by 13 attached towers, equipped with loops and embellished with niches and heraldic plaques, the wall remains one of the most striking features of the burgh and is the longest remaining expanse of medieval walling in Scotland.

and the altar to St Andrew in the south. It was Prior James Haldenstone who established the importance of the Chapel of the Blessed Virgin (the Lady Chapel), in the north side of the choir aisle by promoting at its altar a solemn mass at which he celebrated in full *pontificalia* wearing the mitre which his office had been granted; here too Bishop James Kennedy founded a daily mass for his soul and that of his mother, Mariota Stewart, in 1465.

More years elapsed after Wishart's construction while the central tower was completed, but the lead roofing of the cathedral was stripped away in 1304 by Edward I for use in

munitions for the siege of Stirling — during the Scottish
Wars of Independence. At last Bishop William de Lamberton
(1297—1328) consecrated the cathedral in the presence of
Robert I, the Bruce, on 5 July 1318; the special consecration
crosses can still be seen on the exterior of the choir and south
transept. When the cathedral was all of a piece there would
be twelve consecration crosses, one for each article of the
Creed; these were anointed with holy oil as badges of Christ,
stamping the building with His mark. Already in place too
would be the insignia of the priory (a crowned St Andrews
Cross) and that of the Order of the Augustinians (a Heart
pierced with Crowned Arrows). The dedication of the
cathedral at St Andrews was a symbolic act of the highest
national importance. Bruce was master of the realm, for
Berwick had fallen the same year, and his brother was King
of Ireland; again, it was the seal on Bruce's restored prestige,
and the seal of Lamberton's restored position in the diocese,
although all of these things were soon to be threatened.

The cathedral was now complete and ran to three hundred
and fifty seven feet in its internal length. It had an aisled
nave of twelve bays now, a huge central tower (maybe with a
spire in its original form), north and south transepts with
three chapels each, an aisled choir of six bays, and beyond
the high altar in the reliquary chapel rested the relics of St
Andrew. Indeed the focal point of the whole cathedral was
the high altar and sanctuary. The altar was set against a
screen (which enclosed the Chapel of the Relics) and was to
have a fine mid-fifteenth century altarpiece, provided by
Prior David Ramsay (1462—69). On the altar sat a *textus*
(Gospel book), a gift of Bishop Fothad, velvet cushions used
as book rests, a fine crucifix, silver cruets and the silver
aspersorium; other items would appear too during feast days
when a huge red carpet was laid down in the sanctuary. The
cathedral's silver and gold plate were the gifts of benefactors
down the decades. Before the high altar was said the High
Mass, but it was also a place where important meetings were
held on legal matters. To the right and left of the high altar

stood the lifesize statues of the Blessed Virgin and St Andrew, in the cathedral since at least 1318 and long associated with the Douglas family — indeed the Virgin's statue was known as 'Le Douglas Lady'. Votive lights would always be burning at the feet of these statues.

Beyond that screen which made up the reredos of the high altar was the Chapel of the Relics of St Andrew entered by doors to each side of the altar. In the centre of this chapel was the reliquary containing the bones of St Andrew which would be elevated so as to be seen above the reredos by those sitting in the choir. Herein too would be the cathedral's other main relics and treasures. Very few people were allowed in this area to see the silver-encrusted spear shaft of Alexander I (which was made into a processional cross), the crystal cross from the field of Bannockburn and the reliquary of St Margaret of Scotland.

All of these relics were an enormous security risk and the safety of them was the duty of the sacrist and sub-sacrist, one of whom would always sleep in church. The choir and sanctuary would be protected by iron railings and gates, and stout locked doors, and a close watch was kept for potential thefts; even so there is evidence of some pilgrims opportunistically stealing precious stones and plate from the images and altars whenever they could. Fire was another hazard which had to be monitored by the sacrist and his deputy, particularly on feast days when the cathedral was flooded with light from candles and the cresset lights (a stone with one or more hollows which contained oil and floating wicks). The sacrist and his assistant probably overlooked the sacred areas from a watch-chamber above the choir screen.

Within the south and north transepts were six altars set within their own bays. The three altars in the south transept were probably dedicated to St Margaret of Scotland, St Michael and St Lawrence the Deacon and Martyr of Rome during the persecution of Valerian. It is possible, too, that the north transept contained the altars of two saints dear to

Scotland's clerics, St Thomas the Martyr of Canterbury and St Martin, Bishop of Tours in the fifth century.

The whole of the cathedral pavements were crammed with the tomb slabs of clerics, aristocrats, famous commoners and unknowns, and the tombs of the bishops and archbishops would be the most striking feature of the cathedral after the altars. Many prelates — most of whom would prepare their own tombs years before their deaths — had altar-tombs where prayers could be said for their souls, and the most popular place for their burials was the cathedral chancel (the choir and the sanctuary). Some of the tombs would bear effigies, picked out in bright colours of red, blue, green and gold. In the cathedral museum is the mutilated head of a bishop from a recumbent effigy tomb said by scholars to be that of Bishop Henry Wardlaw (1403−40) which lay in the Lady Chapel.

Heart burials too were popular in medieval times and St Andrews cathedral contained examples: the heart of Bishop William Frazer (who died in Paris in 1297, a refugee from Edward I) was buried in the choir wall beside the tombs of bishops Gamelin and Lamberton. It is curious that although St Andrews cathedral was the most important church in Scotland it had little royal patronage. No kings or queens were interred within St Andrews cathedral, yet one royal personage did have a tomb here. He was James Stewart (*circa* 1479−1504), Duke of Ross and Archbishop of St Andrews, the latter appointment procured (the young archbishop was actually well under the canonical age of appointment of 30) for him by his royal elder brother James IV. In the *Ledger* of Prior Andrew Halyburton we learn that James Stewart's tomb cost £31. 8s 2d (*guldins*). 'The gret stan' of the tomb can still be seen before the site of the Altar of the Relics, almost eleven feet long by five feet, also over five inches thick; set in its upper face was a huge monumental brass with the incised figure of the archbishop. The stone was cleared of rubble in 1826 and shows the level of the cathedral floor in medieval times. In his *History of St Andrews* (1863) the Rev C. J. Lyon

The so-called 'Haunted Tower' in Prior Hepburn's walls, St Andrews Cathedral. The tower got its name from the story of the spectre of the 'White Lady' who is said by the credulous to emerge from the tower. Long used as a burial vault, the tower was opened and its burials examined in 1868 and 1888. Set into the precinct wall are interesting memorials of prominent families in the area.

notes that near to the coffin of James Stewart 'was found a skeleton with a deep cut on the skull as if caused by the heavy blow of a broadsword; and this might be young Archbishop A[*lexander*] Stewart, who received his death-wound at Flodden, and whose remains would, in all probability, be conveyed for interment to his own cathedral church, and buried among his predecessors.' Lyon further notes: 'This skull is still preserved in the museum of St Salvator's college'. Young Alexander was the illegitimate son of James IV and he was appointed to succeed James Stewart as archbishop when he was eleven years old; he died at the Battle of Flodden with his father in 1513.

All of the tombs of the clergy were despoiled and looted at the Reformation, John Knox's rabble rightly presuming that the archbishops, bishops and priors would be buried in full canonicals with personal mass sets of gold and silver, and croziers, jewelled mitres and episcopal rings. Two graves, however, may still contain (the stripped) cadavers of their founders, that of Archbishop William Schevez (1478−96) in the choir and that of William Bell, bishop elect of St Andrews (1332−42) in the south choir aisle.

During the end of the episcopate of William de Landells (1342−85), in 1378, a great fire consumed the cathedral necessitating repair to the choir and transepts. During the episcopates of Walter Trail (1385−1401), Henry Wardlaw (1403−40) and James Kennedy (1440−65), when the university was being founded and state affairs were developing in complexity, the cathedral repairs and maintenance fell heavily on the shoulders of the priors, particularly Prior James Bissett (1396−1416). Indeed the repairs went on for many years; in 1409 the south transept was thrown down in a great storm, adding to complications. Thereafter the work was finished in the days of Prior James Haldenstone (1419−43) who supplied glass lamps, altars and furnishings. There do not seem to be many structural changes to the cathedral after the days of Prior Haldenstone except those of Prior John Hepburn (1482−1522), even taking into consideration that the See of St Andrews was elevated into an archbishopric on 13 August 1472 by Pope Sixtus IV.

Each day pilgrims would arrive at St Andrews bringing with them wealth and income for the cathedral chapter and a lucrative bed and breakfast trade to the citizens, although some pilgrims would camp in the 'square' outside the cathedral's west door, or stay − if they were prominent folk − at the hostel of St Leonard provided for the purpose. St Andrews was the only place outside continental Europe to boast corporeal relics of an Apostle and the draw was great. The pilgrims were, socially both high and low from barons and knights to labourers and the infirm seeking solace from the cares of life and disease within the aura of the bones of *Sancti Apostoli Andreae*; clerics came too, to refresh their faith and one such regular visitor was Guderic the Pirate, who became St Godric the Benedictine founder of Finchale Priory, County Durham.

Although there were several pilgrim routes to St Andrews, the main one was the East Coast route, linking with the pilgrim trails to and from the Shrine of St Cuthbert at Durham. From East Lothian the pilgrim route crossed from North Berwick to Ardross (northeast of modern Elie), Fife, via the *passagium comitis* ('the Earl's ferry') founded in the twelfth century by Duncan, fourth Earl of Fife; hostels for the pilgrims were established at North Berwick and Ardross and the ferry and hostels were run by the Cistercian nuns of the hospital and convent of North Berwick.

From the west they crossed the Forth by the *passagium reginae* ('the Queen's ferry') founded by St Margaret and were succoured at the hostels at each side, and made their way by the King's Road to Cupar and Guardbridge. At the wooden *gair* bridge (replaced in 1419 by a stone bridge by Bishop Wardlaw) they gathered at the neighbouring *statio,* or halting place by the River Eden to travel on to St Andrews in a group under armed guard through the outlaw territory of Kincaple and Strathtyrum marshlands. From the northeast they crossed the Tay by the Ferry of the Loaf from Broughty Ferry to Ferry-Port-on-Craig or to the ferries at Woodhaven, or Balmerino, run by the monks of Abroath Abbey and Balmerino Abbey respectively. The pilgrims were of all nationalities, from Germany and France, Scandinavia and Spain, all mingling with local pilgrims from Fife's towns and villages all seeking pardons for sins.

As we stand today in the ruins of the cathedral it is hard for us to picture the throng of the nave in medieval times. Indeed we would be repelled and sickened by the cluster of wretched cripples writhing down the nave to be as close as they could to the Chapel of the Relics, we would retch at the stench of poverty and diseases and stop our ears at the screams of the insane fettered in chains and cords to the pillars; and all around attention would be distracted for us by the pious noisily mouthing their prayers and offering pennies, marked in the saint's name, mingled with the sounds of the sick vomiting and the dying groaning. On the altar steps, or on a table placed in the nave, the pilgrims would pile their silver and wax images, and a strange collection of gifts — a model arm to be healed, a replica leg that was palsied, a worm that a pilgrim had vomited and piles of homemade candles of thread and animal fat.

The focus of the pilgrim's devotions was the Shrine of the Relics of St Andrew, but few but the mighty would be able to see the relics in their Great Reliquary (*Morbrac*) of Celtic workmanship. At certain times, like the Feast of St Andrew (30 November) and the Coming of the Relics (6 February), the reliquary would be set on its feretory (bier) by the 'dewar', or keeper of the reliquary, and under a canopy it would be processed round the streets after High Mass had been said in its presence at the high altar. Down South Street and up North Street the *Morbrac* would be carried, preceded by masters and scholars from the colleges carrying flowers and leafed branches, while members of the town's guilds would enact religious tableaux and pageants. Around the *Morbrac* the clergy processed in fine vestments and sang hymns to suit the occasion.

By and large the relics were kept under lock and key and constant watch in their own chapel, but they did sometimes leave St Andrews, particularly in time of national emergency: like the time in 1543 when Henry VIII threatened to 'spoyle and turne upset downe the cardinalles town of St Andrews' as a part of his 'rough wooing' of Mary Queen of Scots; this time the relics went for safe keeping to Lochleven castle. What happened to the relics at the Reformation is not known, but it is hardly credible that the canons of the cathedral would not know that the reforming mob were approaching the cathedral with despoliation in their hearts, John Knox had given them enough warning with his hysterical bluster.

So, did the canons secrete the relics in some place? We shall only discover when another miracle occurs. Or, were they spirited out of the country to be returned to Rome? Still, a reputed relic of St Andrew remains in Scotland; Pope John Paul II gave one of the shoulder-blades of the saint to St Mary's Catholic Cathedral at Edinburgh during his visit.

The cathedral was the location for many historical occasions and important meetings. For instance, during June 1538, the marriage of James V with Marie de Guise-Lorraine took place before the high altar. There were pageants devised by Sir David Lindsay and jousting, hunting and banquets on that occasion, and on the morning of her arrival in St Andrews the bride heard conventual High Mass at 10 o'clock. Diocesan synods, presided over sometimes by the archbishop, or sometimes by the vicar-general or substituting commissary, were also held in the cathedral. The synod covered all aspects of ecclesiastical life in the archdiocese. Business of the synod was held in the Senzie (Synod) Hall after mass and a sermon. There was at this time receipt of the parochial dues and the accepting of gifts to the church.

Most of the heresy trials of the diocese were held in the cathedral: on 23 July 1433, Paul Kraver (Craw) was burned at St Andrews after his trial in the cathedral, and during February 1527 Patrick Hamilton was arraigned and at his trial the preacher was Alexander Campbell, Prior of the Blackfriars. Sentence was read by James Beaton in the presence of a great multitude of clergy. In 1533 Henry Forest was burned at the north side of the cathedral so that the people of Forfarshire could see the flames as a deadly warning, and George Wishart was tried in the cathedral before Cardinal Archbishop David Beaton. On 20 April 1558 Walter Myln was tried before Archbishop John Hamilton and the preacher was Simon Maltman, warden of the Greyfriars; this was the last trial held in the cathedral. The trials were looked upon as social occasions, and within the cathedral, probably before the chancel screen, the clergy sat in a specially erected wooden grandstand (*magna scala*); alongside was a pulpit for the red-hooded 'accuser' and the accused spoke from a rostrum. The ordinary folk filled the nave to hear the proceedings.

The end of the cathedral was to come in the mid-sixteenth century when new religious thought was asserting itself out of the fresh theological opinions from the Continent. But there was more to it than that. First there was growing opposition in Scotland to the French influence brought about by the marriage of the Dauphin Francis with Mary Queen of Scots in 1558. The nobility began to work against this alliance, and to avoid being classed as traitorous rebels and potential regicides they invited the exiled John Knox to return to Scotland and they tied in their political cause with his 'godly work'. Then, reform offered an opportunity to work off old family scores and line pockets with the wealth of church properties. Cardinal Beaton was murdered as a retaliation for the execution of George Wishart and the whole thing escalated into a national crisis in which many of the academic clergy, in particular, saw advantage.

So, undermined by its own clergy, the death knell of the cathedral was to be rung on Sunday, 11 June 1559. With the town occupied by the Protestant lords, James, Argyll, Ruthven, Erskine of Dun, Wishart of Pittarrow and others, Knox preached at Holy Trinity Church and continued his rantings for three days, whereupon the work of destruction began on Wednesday, 14 June. Hardly had Knox finished speaking than the mob, orchestrated by the Protestant lords, sacks at the ready to carry off the booty, made for the cathedral 'to purge the kirk and break down the altars and images and all kind of idolatrie. . . .' as the *Historie of the Estate of Scotland* said. The wooden statues were piled in a heap where Myln had been martyred and burned by the followers of the Protestant lords and at their direction. Knox was just whitewashing the acts of vandalism when he said that the cathedral was raped by the St Andreans themselves and with the agreement of their magistrates. Altars, images, tombs, statues were all broken up and the dead robbed of their funeral goods. The buildings of the cathedral were left intact, but on that day four hundred years of continuous worship came to an end. Without doubt, the crypto-Protestant clergy did make off with moveable plate and valuables from the cathedral before the mob came. James Stewart, Earl of Moray, and prior certainly feathered his own nest with cathedral booty, and the cathedral bells, brass lairs, lead, timber, slates and other usable building material would be quickly filtched by all who could carry it away. Indeed the cathedral was used as a quarry right into the eighteenth century.

The books dealing with the muniments (*chartularium*), title-deeds (*carte*), charters of privilege (*privelegia*) of the priory and cathedral have long vanished. It is known that the following existed: the thirteenth century *General cartulary* was added to in the fourteenth century and later, and an eighteenth century transcript of it is in the National Library of Scotland — Sir Alexander Gilmour of Craigmillar possessed certain folios in the seventeenth century and they were in the collection of the Maule family, Earls of Panmure, but disappeared after 1841. Then there was the great *Magnum Registrum.* In 1924 the letterbook of Prior James Haldenstone was re-discovered in the Ducal Library of Wolfenbüttel and was given wide circulation in 1930 as the *Copiale Prioratus Sanctiandree.*

After the Reformation, the chapter of St Andrews remained, as about half of the clergy began to serve the new religion and up to at least 1570 twice-annual meetings were held to discuss the upkeep of the priory and the needs of the 'new clergy'. By 1565 the Lord James Stewart was still living in the priory house and the canons dwelt in their buildings, although there are tales of brutality and intimidation towards them and they were expected to wear secular clothes.

John Hamilton was the last of the medieval Archbishops of St Andrews and he was driven from his See in 1559; Hamilton was executed in 1571 for his alleged part in the assassination of the Regent Moray and the archbishopric was assigned to John Douglas, Principal of St Mary's College.

The position of archbishop remained under attack and was considered irrelevant under presbyterianism, but episcopacy was not abandoned and the title persisted until the appointment of the last Protestant archbishop, Arthur Rose, whose title died with him in 1704. The name of St Andrews disappeared as an ecclesiastical title until 1842 when it was restored as the Bishopric of St Andrews, Dunkeld and Dunblane and still exists within the Episcopal Church in Scotland. When the Roman Catholic hierarchy was restored in 1878 it was decided to utilise St Andrews and Edinburgh in the title of one of the two new Scottish Roman Catholic archbishops and so it remains.

During 1826 the ruins of the cathedral were taken over by the Barons of the Exchequer and excavated, and in 1946 the priory was given over to the then Ministry of Works. The immediate environs to the north and east of the cathedral were used extensively as burial areas and it is known that interments continued in the cathedral nave until 1834. The Chapter House was excavated during 1904—5 and a large amount of coloured window glass was found in the north transept. The markings of the original sites of the pillars of the cathedral nave and the lines of the demolished walls were cut out in the turf in 1888, and in 1988 the long-sealed south processional doorway, from cloister to nave, was reopened.

CHAPTER 4

A Home for Bishops and Archbishops

The rumbustious nature of Scottish medieval politics made it necessary that the bishops of St Andrews have a strong residence. Until the development of St Andrews castle as a fortress, prison and archiepiscopal palace, the bishops had resided at the Augustinian priory. Records show that Bishop Roger de Beaumont, Chancellor of Scotland and erstwhile Abbot of Melrose, who was the son of Robert, Earl of Leicester and cousin of William the Lion, built the first castle here *circa* 1200. Even so, it is likely that the site was some sort of earthen fortification long before Roger's time, set on the pentagonal mini-headland, with its beetling cliffs rising sheer from the Hind Lake. Probably Bishop Malvoisin finished off Roger's work because he was not to enjoy his new palace very long; Roger died at Cambuskenneth on 9 July 1202, and the only part of his castle remaining is the rear of the Fore Tower overlooking the courtyard.

St Andrews castle suffered much in the political jockeyings of the Wars of Independence and Sir William Wallace too. It changed hands several times between the Scots and the English over the next few years. In 1303—04 Edward I held his parliament in St Andrews and was using the castle as a royal residence. Shortly after Bannockburn in 1314, it was occupied and repaired by Edward's stubborn opponent Bishop William de Lamberton. It was taken again by the English in 1332, during the wimpish resistance of David II to the warlike episodes of the pretender to the Scottish throne John Balliol, on behalf of Edward III, and Bishop James de Bone was expelled. The castle was rebuilt in 1336 by the English noblemen Henry de Beaumont and Henry de Ferrers, who, it is said, also rebuilt the Norman castle of the de Quincys at Leuchars. Sir Andrew Moray, Regent of Scotland, besieged

St Andrews castle in 1337 and, reported Wyntoun, 'erd syn dang it doun' as a part of Bruce's scorched earth policy.

St Andrews castle then lay neglected and ruined until 1385 when it was rebuilt from its foundations by the Avignon Pope Clement VII's ambassador or *referendarius,* Bishop Walter Trail of Blebo, and his work is seen particularly in the west range of the castle. During this period the bishops probably resided in the priory and at the Boarhills palace of Inchmurtach.

The early layout of the castle 1200 — 1400 consisted of the bishop's own apartments, to the front with its chapel of 1386; below the chapel were probably the rooms and library of the chaplain with a loggia on the north wall. Two towers were built over the northern cliffs; the Sea Tower (the donjon to the northwest) was the residence of the castle's constable who oversaw the bishop's household and was in charge of the defences, remembering, of course, that artillery was a Crown monopoly and the castle probably had no guns of its own in time of peace; while the Kitchen Tower and its allied chambers dealt with the necessary sustenance of the garrison. Next to the Kitchen Tower was the Seagate which had a slipway down to the sea. The Great Hall (which fell into the sea in 1801) was set within the east range of the castle walls, and all round the landward side of the castle would be the beginnings of a moat.

Within the castle's Sea Tower of Trail's day is the still-extant medieval garderobe and the twenty four foot Bottle Dungeon *circa* 1386. Hollowed out of the solid sandstone, the dungeon is shaped like a bottle with a 'neck' some five feet in diameter and within its damp depths 'many of God's children were imprisoned', says John Knox. Perhaps one of the dungeon's first occupants was Canon Thomas Plater, who had murdered Prior Robert of Montrose in 1393. There are those academics who discard the 'dungeon' idea and argue that the pit was no more than a grain store excavated for Trail's vital supplies. The office of constable, incidentally, was an important perk handed out by the bishop and several prominent Fife families held the position, like the de Wemysses of Kilmany appointed by Bishop Wardlaw.

It was in Trail's new castle that James I was educated by Bishop Wardlaw, James later returned to the castle after English capture and used it as a favourite residence. If we can believe the *Golden Charter* of James II, then his son James III was born here in 1452, and from James's reign the castle was the palace and prison of Patrick Graham, first Archbishop of St Andrews, before he was removed to permanent confinement at Iona, Dunfermline Abbey, and the Isle of St Serf, Lochleven, where he died in 1478. The castle was visited often by Mary of Guelders, spouse of James II.

The violent death of Archbishop Alexander Stewart with his father James IV at Flodden Field in 1513 caused more alarums at the castle. No less than four contenders came forward for the vacant See. There was Gavin Douglas (*circa.* 1474—1522), the poet and ultimately Bishop of Dunkeld, who seized the castle to cement his nomination. Prior John Hepburn was elected by his canons and drove Douglas from the castle. James Beaton, Archbishop of Glasgow, was also nominated as was Andrew Forman, Bishop of Moray, the Pope's nominee who was duly elected. The castle, however, remained in the hands of the Hepburns for a while and Forman resided at Dunfermline.

The great heyday of the castle was undoubtedly during the archiepiscopate of Forman's successor, Archbishop James Beaton (1523—39) for then the fortress was maintained in splendour and the hospitality for visitors was lavish; so much so that the English ambassador commented thus: 'I understand there hath not been such a house kept in Scotland many days before, as of late the said archbishop hath kept, and yet keepeth; insomuch as at the being with him of these lords (Angus, Lennox, Argyle etc), both horses and men, he gave livery nightly to twenty-one score horses.'

Cardinal David Beaton succeeded his uncle as archbishop during 1539—46 and he continued the splendour and from his castle he plotted his opposition to Henry VIII. Beaton refused to ratify the marriage contract which Henry had proposed between his son Edward and the infant Mary, daughter of James V. To persuade the Scots of the desirability of this match Henry conducted the 'rough wooing' and his armies invaded Scotland from 1543. During that time, in 1546, when Beaton was strengthening the castle against a threatened attack events were brewing that were to lose his faction the castle and Beaton his life. To understand the outcome we must introduce George Wishart.

To thwart Beaton, Henry VIII had begun to treat with various lords and gentry who were in dispute with the cardinal, and many of whom like the Earls of Cassillis and Glencairn were known as the 'English Faction'. An intimate associate of this faction was the Protestant fanatical preacher George Wishart (b.*circa* 1513), who loathed Beaton and the Roman Catholic church. But Wishart was more extreme than even Luther or Calvin and considered himself 'God's appointed agent' and received into his circle as a devoted follower another fanatic, John Knox of Haddington.

Beaton soon recognised Wishart as a man dangerous to the medieval church and a demagogue capable of whipping up violence against its officers. Wishart was arrested while preaching at Haddington and was brought to St Andrews, where after four weeks' imprisonment he was tried for heresy on 28 February 1546 on the formal accusation of John Wynram, sub-prior of St Andrews. Wishart was sentenced to death, and was strangled and burned in front of St Andrews castle on 1 March 1546. Today his initials are spelled out in granite blocks on the site of the execution; the setts were placed here in 1946 on the 400th anniversary of his 'martyrdom'.

Before he died, tradition has it, Wishart looked up at the window of the new blockhouse tower which Beaton was having built and caught the eye of the cardinal and his guest Gavin Dunbar, Archbishop of Glasgow, who were watching the immolation begin and said: 'He who in such state, from

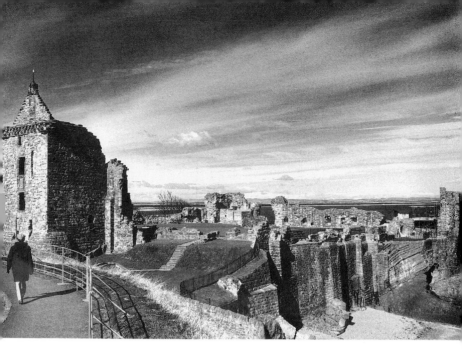

St Andrews Castle from the East Scores. Although the extant work today is largely of the 16th century, the first castle was built *circa* 1200 by Bishop Roger de Beaumont. It was an episcopal and archiepiscopal palace, fortress and state prison. The Fore Tower, to the left, is mainly of the 1336 rebuilding (*Peter Adamson*).

that high place, feedeth his eyes with my torments, within a few days shall be hanged out at the same window, to be seen with as much ignominy, as he now leaneth there in pride.'

For the moment Beaton stood supreme; Wishart had been silenced and Knox was a man hunted from town to town. But conspirators began to gather led by Norman Lesley, Master of Rothes; the Kirkcaldys of Grange joined with the learned James Melville and other Fife lairds to wreak vengeance on the despised cardinal. On 28 May 1546, fifteen or so conspirators gathered in St Andrews and by a clever stratagem entered the castle despite the hundred or so men at arms and the multitude of workmen then at work on the castle frontage. It was all too easy, so it must be presumed that the conspirators had inside help. At last the door was broken down of the cardinal's chamber to which he had fled on seeing his guards and servants melt away. He parleyed with the intruders for a while and despite his admonition that he was a priest, John Lesley and Peter Carmichael hacked at him with their swords and the cardinal was finally dispatched by Wishart's friend James Melville. It is said that the cardinal's body was hung for all to see on the east blockhouse wallhead. Soon the cardinal's body was cut down and pickled in salt and sealed in a kist and placed within the Bottle Dungeon; eventually the cadaver was secretly buried in the chapel of the Blackfriars in South Street.

The Protestants now held the castle and with the help of Henry VIII they retained it for a year. In due time the castle was besieged by the 2nd Earl of Arran, who, supplemented by a French fleet and arms under the command of Leon Strozzi, Prior of Capua, succeeded in capturing the castle which was greatly damaged from cannon mounted on the cathedral tower and on the tower of St Salvator's church.

Still to be seen is a military relic of this siege in the mine and countermine, rediscovered in 1879. This medieval siege work dates from Arran's siege of the castle in which he cut a passageway through the rock (the entrance is beneath the house at the corner of Castle Wynd at the north end of North Castle Street) with the intent of breaching the castle's foundations and thereby gaining entry. The defenders, however, cut an intercepting countermine to thwart this exercise. Today's visitors can clamber through this rare example of the medieval sappers' work. These mines gave rise to many a Victorian 'secret passage' story, and Dean of Guild Linskill was a keen promoter of them; not every academic accepts the mine and countermine theory so maybe there is some truth in the secret passage story after all!

The castle is known to have been rebuilt by Cardinal Beaton's successor Archbishop John Hamilton, and his armorial cinquefoil (a five-pointed star) is seen above the present (in fact the fourth) entrance gateway; his heraldic panel is also to be seen on the front wall of the Fore Tower

Part of the mine and countermine cut through the rock at the outside south-east base of the Fore Tower of St Andrews Castle. The mine was a part of the sappers' siege technique during the assault on the Castle of 1546—47. The entrance to the mine is under the house called Castlegate (1879), North Castle Street corner, while the countermine is entered from the castle ditch.

between two windows. By Hamilton's day the buildings of the castle were complete; from the entrance with its vaulted guard rooms and postern door the frontage runs west to lead to the west blockhouse of 1544. A suite of four rooms comprised the frontage, the west elevation overlooking the bishop's garden (a part of the grounds of Castlecliff, 1877); joining the curtain wall to the Sea Tower and the Kitchen Tower were the 'gentlemen's appartments' where the Great Hall joined the chapel to the east blockhouse.

It is certain that towards the close of 1559 the castle was in the hands of the Protestant Reformers who would cleanse it of 'idolaterie' and vestiges of the medieval churchmen who lived there; indeed an inventory of 1565 shows that it was very scantily furnished by that date. In 1583 James VI escaped from capture by the Ruthvens of Huntingtower and took shelter in the castle, and in 1587 the castle passed, through the Act of Annexation, and along with other church property, to the Crown. During 1606 the king granted it to George Home, later Earl of Dunbar. By 1612 the castle had reverted to the archbishopric and it was repaired by the (Episcopal) Archbishop George Gledstanes who lived in it until his death in 1615. Archbishop Spottiswoode was complaining that the castle was ruinous in 1629 and he removed his quarters to the *Hospitium Novum* in 1635. By then the office of constable had fallen into desuetude. Parliament ordered the St Andrews Town Council to repair the castle in 1645 and it was used as a state prison a year later. In 1654 the Town Council ordered that part of the castle stone work be used to repair the harbour and in 1656 castle slate and timber were sold to defray the expense of repairing the Long Pier.

It is interesting to note how the environs of the castle have changed greatly since the seventeenth century; writing in 1693, George Martine states that in his time people remembered how bowls were played on the level ground to the east and north of the castle; and Francis Grose in 1791 quoted old sources to say that the proprietor of the neighbouring estate 'had the privilege of driving his cattle and goods on the east side of the castle'. During the period 1724 to 1808 the castle 'close' was rented to various individuals and in 1802 Principal Playfair made an appeal for restoration of the castle, the tenant of the courtyard having closed the castle gate and 'ploughed up the area and planted potatoes on several parts of the ruins'. A keeper was first appointed in 1810. In 1857 the castle well was rediscovered and in 1864–65 the moat was cleared out. The walls abutting the sea were given protection walls in 1884–86, 1892 and 1903 and by 1904 the Castle Beach bathing pond was established, although the beach hereabouts had been used for bathing for some considerable time. In 1911 the castle was taken into government custody and guardianship as an ancient monument.

When in residence in St Andrews, the bishops' and archbishops' households were very large; the archbishops, for instance, ruled a realm within a realm from Kincardine to Lothian and had command over the spiritual and secular lives of around 80,000 souls in medieval times. To run the archdiocese from St Andrews castle they had hundreds of staff from clerks to masons, gunners to cooks, musicians to brewers, bodyservants to tailors and apothecaries to men-at-arms. The archbishop's representatives were all seeing and had no doors closed to them. Many of the plum jobs on the bishop's and archbishop's staff were secured through nepotism, but the princes of the church employed a wide range of local people from the lairds to the artisans of the burgh.

One of the rare functions of a Scottish bishop was to act as coiner, and Bishop James Kennedy carried out his coining at St Andrews castle. Kennedy had been granted by charter the privilege of striking coins by James II in 1452 and these coins today are very rare and much sought after by collectors. Of the pennies coined at St Andrews for Bishop Kennedy the obverse bears an orb with a cross breaking through the legend to act as a mintmark. This is surrounded by royal titles: *Iacobvs Dei Gra [tia] Rex* – 'James by the Grace of God King'. On the reverse a Latin cross in a tressure of four arcs appears with the motto *Crux Pellit Omne Crimen*, the first line of the vesper hymn *Ante Somnum* by Prudentius. Kennedy's

St Andrews farthings were copied, numismatists state, from the 'black farthings' of James III, which had already appeared in the early 1470s. The reverse design is quite original bearing a long cross pattée with six-pointed mullets and crowns in alternate angles: the reverse inscription reads *Mone* [*ta*] *Paup* [*erum*], for 'money of the poor'. The design of Kennedy's coins can compare closely with the work on the mace of St Salvator's College and knowledge of them dates back to 1919 when a hoard of them were found at the Abbey of Crossraguel, Ayrshire. Kennedy's coins had a wide circulation in the east of Scotland, and are a rare treasure for they form the only medieval coins of the whole of Great Britain not only to have been struck by the authority of a primate, but which also bear his own arms. It is interesting to note that coins were minted at St Andrews castle under Alexander III (1241 – 86) and John Baliol (1250 – 1313), the former bearing the name of Thomas the Minter and the latter the name of the burgh, boldly and clearly.

CHAPTER 5

The Burgh, Guilds, Visitors and Townsfolk

The development of St Andrews as a burgh began some time between 1144 and 1153, when it was raised into such status by Bishop Robert with the active enthusiasm and permission of David I. The word *burgh* (or *burg*) originally meant a fortified place, where people could group to resist attack by an enemy, and as time went by two main types of burgh developed in Scotland, Royal Burghs and Burghs of Regality and Barony. The former were burghs directly founded by the king, and those on the lands of a subject superior, be they cleric or layman. David I gave charters to twelve burghs, which he called *meo burgo* and included St Andrews' neighbour of Crail, while St Andrews itself was in its origin a Bishop's Burgh. In 1614 St Andrews was made a Burgh of Regality under the Archbishop of St Andrews, and King James VI made it into a Royal Burgh in 1620. When his burgh was established Bishop Robert looked south to Berwick for his first provost (*praepositus*): Berwick had been made a royal burgh *circa* 1120 by David I and was one of the Court of Four Burghs (*Curia Quattuor Burgorum*), and the See already had some properties in Berwick and drew rent from burgages. Bishop Robert chose the opulent wool merchant (*proprius burgensis*), Maynard the Fleming, as St Andrews' first provost.

If we look at a charter of Bishop Richard (1163–78) we can see that the early heart of St Andrews was in that area including North Castle Street, South Castle Street (once Hucksters' Wynd), part of the narrow end of Market Street and the site of Nos 19–21 North Street; probably the focal point of the secular St Andrews was the fortification that pre-dated Bishop Roger's castle. Once the cathedral was established the second phase of the burgh development took place and by 1260 South Street as far as modern Bell Street would be laid out, with Market Street and North Street to approximately the New Picture House (1930), North Street being an extension of the route into the old Bishop's Burgh and South Street being a thoroughfare planned to lead directly into the cathedral precinct. The development of early housing at modern Gregory Place, Deans Court and the east end of South Street and Abbey Street would be within the barony of the priory and the archdeacon, outwith the original burgh.

By 1560 the burgh had developed to modern Murray Place, and the West Port. It may be remembered too that the area of Argyll Street to modern Alfred Place (once Cow Wynd) was a separate development, called Argyle, outwith the medieval burgh and had been a part of its neighbour Rathelpie, which stretched as far as Priory Acres. Rathelpie may have been a fortified Pictish settlement and the lands were ultimately in the endowment of the Hospital of St Leonard. Argyle — from *Earra Ghaidheal* 'borderland of the Gael' — where lived the folk called 'Pachlers', seems to have been a village of thatched houses for people who at first won their living from the land and became mostly stone masons in the summer and handloom weavers in the winter. The hamlet developed to have seven dairies and two bakehouses and a public house called the Thacket Inn owned by one Adam Dick whose sign once read:

> Adam Dick of the Thacket Inn
> Sells ale and whisky
> But nae gin.

Within Argyle too was a chaplain's house and probably a residence of Gavin Dunbar, archdeacon of St Andrews 1504—19. On the northern boundary of Argyle is sited castellated Kinburn House, built for the Buddos in 1854—56 on the land bought in 1852 by Dr David Buddo of the Indian Medical Service. St Andrews Town Council acquired the house — named after a Russian fort captured by a Franco-

British naval force during the Crimean War — in 1920 from the descendants of Provost John Paterson of St Andrews. The clock on the southeast tower, incidentally, was set up in 1948 as a memorial to Miss McLaren. Around the house today is a public park, bowling green and tennis courts, the location of many Scottish Hard Court Championships.

The key social units in medieval St Andrews were the burghers, usually family men, with, perhaps, a dependant relative or two living under their roofs. The burgher was himself the most important townsman, with the stallagers (market stall holders who enjoyed fewer burgh privileges and paid fewer dues on property and trade) next, followed by the journeymen, the labourers and the servants each with their own families. At the bottom of the heap were the poor, the disabled and the chronically sick, the lepers and the beggars all of whom looked to the religious orders for their aid.

As far as the burghers were concerned the centre of the medieval town was the tolbooth, the Scottish equivalent of the English town hall where taxes were collected. When they demolished the old tolbooth — once set in Market Street near to the modern site of the Whyte-Melville Memorial Fountain — in 1862 it was observed that there had been four buildings on the site, with the first dating from soon after the granting of the royal burgh status of *circa* 1144. The tolbooth, which developed as a two-storey building with an outside stone stair that was removed *circa* 1818, contained a police cell, a debtor's prison and a 'thief's hole'. Facing the east were the hustings where parliamentary candidates addressed their electors, and on the tolbooth wall were the *jougs* (removed *circa* 1830), an instrument of punishment in the form of a collar to be placed around the miscreant's neck. The tolbooth was not used as a state prison as was the castle, but David Calderwood, the Presbyterian historian, was imprisoned in the tolbooth in 1617. Subscriptions for the upkeep of the tolbooth came from such as the Seven Incorporated Trades, the Royal Arch Masons, the Thistle and

Rose Free Gardeners Lodge, and the Royal & Ancient Golf
Club, which allowed these bodies to use the civic chambers
for meetings down the decades. The tolbooth bell was recast
in 1697 by John Meikle of Edinburgh and bore the inscription:
CURA-IA-SMITH-MAG-ALEX-NAIRN-GEO-RAYNER-
IO-CRAIG-1697-BALNORVM-CIVITATIS-STI-ANDRAE
IN-CVRRARVM-VSVM-SVM:REFVSVS-IO-MEIKLE-ME-
FECIT-EDINBVRGH. '(Erected) under the administration
of James Smith, Mr Alexander Nairn, George Rayner, and
John Craig, Bailies of the City of St Andrews, to be rung in
all the Courts, 1697. Recast and manufactured by John Meikle
at Edinburgh.' A new town hall containing this bell in the
corner turret was built at St Andrews in the Scottish baronial
style during 1858—61 at the head of Queens Gardens (then
Queens Street) on the site of the shop belonging to Melville
Fletcher & Sons, booksellers; the foundation stone for the
town hall was laid with full masonic honours by Past Grand
Master for Fife and Kinross John Whyte-Melville (1821—78);
the town hall was reconstructed in 1968.

The Mercat Cross and the Public Weigh Beam (known as
the Tron) stood in front of the tolbooth in a line with the
entries to Church Street and College Street into the square.
The Mercat Cross has six circular pyramidal steps with a
ten—twelve feet obelisk used as a pillory. At the Mercat
Cross Paul Craw, the physician cum Hussite social
revolutionary was burned at the stake in 1433 with a brass
ball stuffed in his mouth to stop him addressing the crowd;
Sir Robert Spottiswoode, Lord President of the Council and
three other royalists were beheaded here in 1646; and Samuel
Rutherford (*circa* 1600—61), Professor of Divinity, whose
book *Lex Rex* of 1644 argued for the right of the people
to depose their king, was burned here in 1660. The Mercat
Cross was removed in 1768, but later royal proclamations
were read from a temporary rostrum on the site; here Queen
Elizabeth II was proclaimed on Saturday, 9 February 1952.

At the Public Weigh Beam the weights and measures of
the day were exhibited and used to assure fair play when

The West Port, the only surviving gateway into the heart of St Andrews. This semi-octagonal bastioned gateway was reconstructed in 1589 by the Blebo mason John Robertson, who modelled it on the Edinburgh Netherbow Port. Renovated in 1843–45, when the side arches were also inserted, the west side of the port carries the plaque depicting King David I with spear in hand, flanked by a bishop and an attendant. The east side plaque shows the arms of the burgh.

commodities were being bought and sold. As with other parts of Scotland, St Andrews had a mixture of weights in the Middle Ages: *English pounds* (16oz avoirdupois) were used for weighing flour, bread and pot-barley; *Dutch pounds* (17½ oz avoirdupois) were used for animal meat and meal; while *Tron pounds* (22 oz avoirdupois) were used for wool, butter, flax, cheese, tallow, hides and hay. A Scottish stone always consisted of 16 lbs and for many years the old Scots terms were widely used by the merchants, such as *boll* (8 stone), *firlot* (2 stone), *peck* (8 lbs) and *lippie* (92 lbs), for peas, beans and so on.

At the Reformation the two- to four-storey merchants' houses of stone predominated in the burgh set on the site of two-storey stone and timber dwellings evolved by the twelfth century with their 'lang riggs' or long-strip holdings. The houses, set on the street front, ran back to the limits of the burgh. At the front of the house the *foreland* abutted the street and here the merchants carried on their trade; behind and reached by a *pend* (passage) through the building were the courtyard of the house and the pleasure and kitchen gardens, the latter known as the *kailyard*. A good place to see the line of the old lang-riggs is from the junction of Queens Terrace with Greenside Place. Number 49 South Street is a good example of a renovated Merchants House with its fine painted ceilings still intact; the property belonged to the Covenanter Robert Blair, one of those who signed the Solemn League and Covenant in 1638 and who preached at Charles II on his visit to the burgh; it is said that Charles actually visited the house. As the burgh became more prosperous a higher density of population would be accommodated in the 'close developments' of the riggs and wynds which linked the old streets with crowded conditions in particular at Logie's Lane (once Coffin Row) and Baker Lane. At the 'back o'the toun', at the end of the lang-riggs, crofts would be built where farming went on at such sites as the Burgh Crofts (modern City Road and Pilmour Links) and Priory Acres. Nearly every one of St Andrews' medieval houses had its own well.

There is no evidence that St Andrews was ever a walled city, but in the sixteenth century the outer extremities of all the streets and wynds were closed by ports or gates. There were, for instance, small gateways at Westburn Wynd, Abbey Wynd and Butts Wynd, with four main town gateways. On the Scores outside St Salvator's Hall can be seen the remains of the buttress of the Swallowport of medieval Swallowgait, which was probably finally demolished in the storm of 1698. Northgait port stood just west of the New Picture House and was demolished in 1838; Northgait had stone balls set on the gateway pillars. Outside Northgait stood a large stone known as the 'Knocking Stone', where the handloom weavers of the 1840s 'knocked' their yarn.

Marketgait Port stood a few yards west of the junction of Greyfriars Garden and Bell Street and abutted the line of the garden of the Greyfriars monastery, and the Old Cow's Pool. The only remaining port of the burgh is the West Port. Called 'Argailles Port' in 1560 it was remodelled from an older gateway in 1589 and completely renovated in 1843 and 1950; its style was based on the now vanished Netherbow Port at Edinburgh and it is one of the two remaining Scots town gateways (the other is Wishart's Arch, or Cowgait Port at Dundee). In 1843 the gateway's two guard-houses were replaced by buttresses. The panel on the gateway shows David I and was inserted in 1843 and is the work of local mason Balfour Simmers and cost £5. 8s 6d (£5.42½p). At this gateway James VI was welcomed to the town on 11 July 1617 and was greeted by the public orator with a Latin address; the silver keys of the old burgh were delivered to Charles II in 1650, a ceremony not to be repeated until 1922 when the keys were offered to the then Prince of Wales (later Edward VIII), on the occasion when the freedom of the burgh was conferred on him. The original Southgait Port of twelfth century date probably was situated just east of Blackfriars.

The commercial life of medieval St Andrews was regulated by the trade guilds, the town's equivalent of the European trade associations which set standards of quality of goods, terms of employment, mutual benefit privileges in time of sickness and so on. St Andrews had the famous Seven Trades of the Bakers, Fleshers, Shoemakers, Smiths, Tailors, Weavers and Wrights and this was a sister organisation of the Guildry which was the medieval local government administration. The Seven Trades regulated the work of their members in the burgh and could effectively stop any 'outsiders' from setting up rival businesses. For a fee of £20, each member of the Trades enjoyed the wide privileges of membership protection; the members wore gold medals to church on Sunday, sat in reserved pews and each had a livery for his trade which was worn on feast days and market days. The Trades owned land at Priory Acres, for instance, and existed as an entity until the early days of Queen Victoria.

The work of the Hammermen of St Andrews always attracted attention; this group included the town's armourers, saddlers, watchmakers, glovers, cutlers, pewterers and smiths. The hammermen were a well-established trade by 1394 — the year that one of the guild brethren, William Plummer, was indentured by John Geddie, Abbot of Arbroath, to repair the abbey roof — and remained as an identifiable trade association until the late eighteenth century. The Hammermen also included the gold and silversmiths and one Patrick Gairden is known to have been working in gold in the sixteenth century; St Andrews silver is very rare, but examples with the distinctive hallmark of the Saltire are to be found in the collection of St. Mary's College.

The markets of St Andrews were the centre of economic life and on the town's market days the country folk would sell their produce and buy their own necessities. In time Mondays and Thursdays developed as St Andrews market days and the range of goods was wide to suit the medieval family, so on any one market day it would be possible to buy: barley, meat, spirits, flax, soap, candles, yarn, locks, hinges, starch, butter, bread, snuff, tobacco, ropes, nails, scythes and reaping-hooks, and arrange for funerals. Local coal was also sold and St Andrews nearly had its own coal mines. On 8 September 1785 a proposition was drawn up between Alexander Duncan of St Fort, Provost of St Andrews, William Landale, Dean of Guild *et al*, to give permission to interested parties to mine for coal at Pilmour Links and North Haugh, but nothing came of the venture.

Outside the east gable of St Andrews tolbooth stood the Buttermarket where a weekly dairy products market was held up to the 1860s. The town had many dairy farms within its bounds at such places as Claybraes, Argyle Farm, Abbey

Lammas Fair, South Street, St Andrews, 1947. A relic of the old Celtic Festival of Autumn, known as Lunasdal, the market remembers the feast 'of the fruits of the soil'. Once a hiring fair, this St Andrews celebration, the oldest surviving medieval fair in Scotland, remains a noisy, brash and colourful spectacle (*The Estate of G. M. Cowie*).

Place, Westburn Lane, Kinnessburn Road and so on. The *St Andrews Gazette* of 1868 reminds us too of the town's Linseed Market, 'once the greatest fair in the city, when every one had to sow their peck and spin their quantity'; lint or flax seed was grown locally and its byproducts were cattle food and oil, the flax itself being made into linen cloth. This market had fallen into disuse by 1870.

Up to Victorian times Handsel Monday was still celebrated in St Andrews on the first Monday of the New Year, and formed a holiday for domestic servants and farm workers. Its name comes from the old Scots word for gift or tip and often took the form of a celebration meal subscribed for by employers. With its beginnings before the Reformation, when the priors gave gifts to the poor after Christmas, Handsel Monday's main attraction in St Andrews was a market selling candles and fruit.

Far more important than these markets were the five great annual fairs: Candlemas; the Easter Senzie Fair; Lammas; Martinmas; and, St Andrew's Day. The book *Delineations of St Andrews* (1838) tells us that only three fairs had survived by Victoria's days.

St Andrews' only surviving fair is the Lammas Market and it is likely that this is the oldest surviving medieval market in Scotland. Lammas, by the by, was the Lunasdal, the Celtic Festival of autumn to honour the fruits of the soil. A delightful anachronism that clogs South Street and the middle of Market Street on the second Monday and Tuesday of August, Lammas Market was secured as a privilege for the burghers in 1620 by James VI & I and was confirmed by Act of Parliament under Charles I. Lammas (or, Loaf Mass) Market was once a one-day hiring fair and an occasion of religious observance which brought a huge influx of people, and until 1800 or so it was the only place where people could buy ironmongery. By the 1870s it had been extended to include Tuesdays. The focal point of the fair was a beer tent at the corner of South Street and Queens Gardens where the hiring of farm workers took place for the ensuing year or half year. The Town Band played all day, with increasing visits to the beer tent as the day progressed. All the public houses in St Andrews did a roaring trade and at the end of the market the roads from the burgh became congested with a rustic crowd bearing only too prominently evidence of the riotous excess of pub and gin-house. Today it is a colourful cacophony of street barkers and fairground features, electric generators taking over from the steam engines and horsepower of Victorian times. Another bright occasion, St Andrews Horse Fair, was wound up after 1952.

One very interesting group of medieval property owners in St Andrews were the Order of the Knights of the Hospital of St John in Jerusalem, a quasi-military religious order sworn to defend the pilgrim routes to the Holy Land and give succour to the pilgrims, the sick and the poor. We first hear of these knights in 1160 in St Andrews, when a charter was witnessed by two of their number namely 'Richard of the Hospital of Jerusalem' and 'Richard, brother of the Temple'. Rather confusingly there were two groups of such knights, the Knights Templars and the Knights Hospitallers. The Templars had two headquarters in Scotland at Balantrodoch, Midlothian, and at Maryculter, Kincardine, while the Hospitallers had only one house, their Preceptory, at Torphichen in West Lothian. After the Templars were disbanded (or suppressed) at the end of the thirteenth century their properties were absorbed by the Hospitallers.

The two groups of knights had tenements off and in North Street, one of which stretched back to Swallowgait, with the properties of numbers 47, 49, 68 — 72 North Street and 45 — 53 Market Street. Nos 67 — 71 South Street, abutting Baker Lane, belonged first to the Templars and then to the Knights of St John. Nos 67 — 69 are now known as St John's and were bought by the university in 1970 for use as a graduate centre for advanced historical studies; the building is perhaps the oldest standing town building in St Andrews, its earliest phase dating from the 15th century on the site of medieval timber buildings. The knights, of course, were never resident in St Andrews; their premises were a source of revenue and their tenants paid their dues to the knights and then to secular landlords after the Reformation and these landlords received the monies up to *circa* 1820 when the town took over the superiority of the properties. By the sixteenth century the properties of St John's and No 71 South Street (now the Dept of Medieval History) were owned by Patrick Adamson, Archbishop of St Andrews (1575–92), and then by his son of the same name; by then the castle was too dilapidated to be an archbishop's residence. Today the frontage of St John's displays the arrangement of former windows and doors.

As the canons of the cathedral knew well from their holy texts, the Old Testament is full of plagues, including the plagues that afflicted Pharaoh's people before Moses was allowed to lead the Israelites out of Egypt. Plague devastated St Andrews burgh from time to time, but the term is confusing as in medieval times it included everything from bacillary dysentery to the dreaded bubonic plague which spread from Asia to Europe during the fourteenth century. It arrived first in Sicily in 1347, and spread rapidly through Italy to the rest of Europe where its devastating effects earned it the name of the Black Death. The Black Death reached England in the summer of 1348, at Melcombe Regis (now a part of Weymouth, Devon) and ecclesiastical records show that twenty-four canons of St Andrews priory died of plague in 1350 and that in 1362 Bishop Landells and his senior clergy fled the burgh, the bishop going to Moray to escape the scourge. The exodus of cathedral officials undoubtedly sowed the seeds which led to the decline of the church's popularity in the burgh — together with the low standards of many of the newly appointed priests — and the fact that belief in God had signally failed to arrest the progress of the Black Death.

After the Black Death, plague was endemic in Britain for 300 years. In 1529, 1568 and 1585 St Andrews was again wracked with plague, the severity of the 1585 epidemic causing the dispersal of students and contributing, because of its duration, to the increase in poverty in the burgh; indeed in 1529 Edinburgh folk were forbidden to travel to St Andrews lest the plague spread to the capital. There were four hundred deaths reported in St Andrews in 1585, and the state of sickness was much aggravated by the wet harvest that year. Plague came to the burgh again in 1605, 1647, 1665 and 1667; in 1647 the Principal of St Leonard's College died of the rat or flea borne bacillus *Yersinia pestis*. The burgh's plague pits were almost certainly located just west of St James's church on the Scores. Bones were discovered here in 1906, 1909 and in 1987 when the Marina was being built (remembering, of course, that the cliffs at the Step Rock were dumping grounds for fragmented bones and rubbish from the sites of Blackfriars and Greyfriars monasteries during the nineteenth century redevelopments).

Before the Reformation witchcraft appears to have been noticed little in Scotland as the medieval church had no Inquisition in the country. If any such cases appear on record culminating in the execution of sorcerers the indictment was not for witchcraft *per se*, but for murder or attempted murder. Again up to the end of the fifteenth century death sentences supposed to have been passed for witchcraft were really on an indictment of heresy for acts said to have been promulgated by magic. Further, a few cases of supposed witchcraft mentioned in the old chronicles can be easily dismissed as a charge of witchcraft being used as a political tool, as in the case of the execution by burning of Jane, Lady Douglas, sister of the Earl of Angus, widow of John, Lord Glamis in 1537. When the Protestant Reformation came, however, the Scriptures were scoured for passages that backed up the politics of the new regime. The quote in *Exodus, xxii, 18.*, 'Thou shalt not suffer a witch to live' gave the Presbyterian politicians the impetus to support the *Acta Parliamentorum Mariae* of 1563 which made witchcraft an illegal act and win for themselves an important legal lever against their enemies and helped confirm the ordinary folk in their credulity.

Scotland had three great periods of witchcraft persecution, 1590—97, 1640—44, and 1660—63 and St Andrews burgh was the scene of some of the witch trials. In truth there were few executions for witchcraft in St Andrews out of the 4000 or so capital indictments in Scotland during 1590 to 1680. From the *Diurnal of remarkable occurrents, Register of the Kirk Session of St Andrews, 1559—1650, Register of the Privy Council, Selection from minutes of the Synod of Fife, 1611—1687,* and the *Rentale Sancti Andree 1538—1546* the following are the best attested cases.

In 1569 the sorceress Nic Neville was condemned and burned, says the *Historie and life of King James the Sext,* but other sources call the same person Nick Niven and make the witch male. In this year too the Regent 'causit burne certane witches in Sanctandrois', and William Sterat, Lyon King of Arms, was hanged for 'necromancie'. During 1572 a witch, personally condemned by John Knox, was burned in the burgh, but the supposed witch Marjorie Smith was charged and accused by the Presbyterian Kirk Session of witchcraft, but it is not known for sure whether or not she was consigned to the flames. Bessy Robertson was charged with witchcraft in 1581 as was Agnes Melville in 1588, but Melville survived until 1595 when she was executed along with Elspeth Gilchrist and Janet Lochequoir. On 30 Sept 1613 a presentation was made to the archbishop accusing Agnes Anstruther of witchcraft, but we hear no more about witch accusations until 1630 which saw the trial of Margaret Callender. In 1644 one Bessie Mason 'a confessing witche' was interviewed by the Synod as was 'the woman called Seweis' in 1645. The last recorded case of witchcraft in St Andrews seems to be the accusation of Isobel Key in 1667 who was imprisoned in the tolbooth, although David Hay Fleming talks of the 'last witch burned in St Andrews being one Young in Market Street' *circa* 1700. When the Statutes against witchcraft in Great Britain were repealed in 1736 many St Andrews Presbyterians were outraged. At the Step Rock (so named after 1835) the visitor can still look east along the cliffs

The frontage of Queen Mary's House, South St, St Andrews. The original structure was built by Augustinian canon Alan Meldrum, Vicar of Leuchars, *circa* 1525, and takes its name from the tradition that Mary Queen of Scots lodged here in 1562 and possibly on later occasions. It is thought that Charles II lodged here too during 4–6 July 1650. The house was opened as a library for St Leonard's school in 1927 and was expanded within for similar use in 1977.

towards St James's church to the site of the Witch Lake where tradition has it witches were 'tested' (by water ordeal) until the late seventeenth century.

The medieval burgh of St Andrews had one celebrated visitor whose name is attached to an important burgh building. Mary, Queen of Scots, visited St Andrews five times during 1561–65, her last visit being in the company of her husband, Henry Stuart, Lord Darnley, a short while before his murder. Wherever she went, the crowds acted with enthusiasm. Apart from anything else Mary made a striking figure in her rich, black dresses with their lace trimmings and billowing skirts. She was a fashion plate of her day and her collection of jewellery was breathtaking. Mary was every inch a queen, and she had inherited all of the legendary Stuart charm. The St Andrews crowds who gathered to see her saw her as a beautiful and enchanting woman first, and as a Roman Catholic queen second. But one must remember that in the crowds that gathered in St Andrews were *agents provocateurs* during her first visit on Sunday, 21 September 1561, for Knox's creatures followed her watching her every move and inciting the crowd against her. That well-respected historian David Hay Fleming tells us that on that day a priest was assassinated in St Andrews, as a chastening example of the new Protestant regime.

Mary's motives in coming to St Andrews were several. She was interested in a closer look at some of the ancient royal burghs in her kingdom, and she was keen to visit her half-brother the Lord James Stewart, Commendator of St Andrews priory. James Stewart, Earl of Moray, was the illegitimate son of Mary's father James V and Margaret Erskine. For the most part we have to rely on oral tradition as to where she stayed in St Andrews. During her visit of 1561 she is likely to have lodged with her half-brother who had apartments in the *Hospitium Novum*, or she may have stayed at the Prior's House. There are no written records to tell us if she stayed at the castle, and her subsequent main residence was the building we now know as Queen Mary's House, South Street.

Queen Mary's House is a particularly fine example of a sixteenth century Scottish town house. Although it has been greatly altered and extended by later owners, much remains of the original structure, and the cellars have changed the least. The house was built by Alan Meldrum, Vicar of Leuchars and Canon of the Priory, in 1525, on land that was the property of the priory; this land had been inhabited from the twelfth century as a part of Kilrimont's policies and by the fourteenth century it was a cultivated field, with a heather thatched timber house of the early fifteenth century. In Meldrum's day there was probably a wooden gallery projecting into South Street. The West Wing was built around 1575 by David Orme, Chamberlain to the Lord James. An East Wing (Priorsgate) dates from around 1580 and was reconstructed *circa* 1792.

During her visit of March to May 1562, Mary welcomed into her presence the English ambassador to the Scottish Court, Sir Thomas Randolph, and it is from his reports that we can build up a picture of Mary's activities in St Andrews. We know for certain that she took part in archery competitions at Smalmonth, the name of a nearby sward, and that she may have shot at the butts too at 71 South Street. She also spent time riding and she did some gardening. Her intellectual pursuits included studying Livy under the tutorship of the Principal of St Leonard's College, George Buchanan. Sir Thomas Randolph was with the queen again in 1565, when he was waiting for Mary's answer to the proposal that she marry the Earl of Leicester. Sir Thomas wrote thus to his mistress Elizabeth I: 'Her grace lodged in a "merchant's house", her train very few and small repair from any part. Her will was that I should dine and sup with her. . . . Having thus spent Sunday, Monday, and Tuesday I thought it time to utter to her grace your majesty's command (*ie, concerning the proposed marriage*). . . . I had no sooner spoken these words but she said: "I see now well that you are weary of this company and treatment: I sent for you to be merry and to see how like a bourgeois wife I live with my little troop"'. . . . 'very merrily she passed her time'.

Although the town still had an archbishop in John Hamilton, he had no ecclesiastical authority in the realm and Mary had to worship while in St Andrews with discretion. Mass had been discontinued in all the town churches following the Acts of 1560, so she set up an Oratory at the South Street House to hear Mass in private; the Lord James had defied the new protestants in their bid to stop Mary worshipping according to the Roman rule.

It is thought that Charles II lodged at Queen Mary's House when he visited the burgh during 4–6 July 1650, and at that time the house seems to have belonged to Hugh

Scrimgeour, servitor to John Spottiswoode, Archbishop of St Andrews. The house passed from church administrators to secular gentry families like James Lumisdaine of Rennyhill, who owned the property from the 1750s to 1785. The house and gardens were sold in 1926, by the widow of the last private owner Captain Nunneley, to St Leonard's School and rooms were laid out for a school library opened in October 1927 by the then Duchess of York (later HM Queen Elizabeth the Queen Mother), who returned in 1977 to open the junior library.

No comment on Mary Stuart in St Andrews would be complete without a mention of the French poet and swaggering galliard Pierre De Boscose de Châtelard who came to Scotland in Mary's entourage in 1561. He was sent, it appears, to Scotland by his employer Seigneur Montmorency d'Amville, for what purpose is not known. In time Châtelard acquired a deep infatuation for Mary and secreted himself in her bedchamber at Holyrood. He was discovered and Mary hysterically demanded that her half-brother run the young man through; Lord James cautiously soothed the queen and Châtelard was admonished and told to leave court. Châtelard followed Mary on a trip to Fife in 1563 and when the queen paused at Rossend Castle, Burntisland, for the night, Châtelard again secreted himself in the queen's bedroom. He said he had come to apologise when he was discovered once more. This was serious *lése majesté* and Châtelard was brought to trial and locked up in St Andrews castle. He was condemned to death on 22 February 1563 and was taken to the scaffold, then sited in Market Street. He declined the consolation of the new church of Scotland, and instead recited, says the chronicler Brantôme, some lines from the poet Pierre Ronsard's 'Hymn to Death' . . . . . .

Je te salue, heureuse et profitable mort . . . .
. . . . puisqu'il faut mourir
Donne-moi que soudain je te puisse encourir
Ou pour l'honneur de Dieu, ou pour servir mon Prince . . . .

(I salute you, happy and profitable Death . . . .
. . . . since I must die
Grant that I may suddenly encounter you
Either for the honour of God, or in the service of my
Prince.)

As the hangman put the noose around his neck Châtelard is
said to have shouted to the crowd: 'Adieu, the most beautiful
and most cruel princess of the world'. It was a pretty harsh
sentence for a flirtatious adventure of a lovesick fool, but
there were those who believed that Châtelard may have been
up to much more. Randolph reported to his royal mistress in
London the whispers that Châtelard was part of a plot to
assassinate Mary. . . . but the truth is never likely to be
known.

The heyday of St Andrews was undoubtedly the time
when it was a prosperous medieval burgh, the ecclesiastical
capital of Scotland. At the Reformation the whole focus of
power, political and commercial, moved from St Andrews to
Edinburgh and Glasgow, and St Andrews never again
achieved its former prosperity. From the jottings of visitors
we begin to see something of the declining city. In 1732 John
Loveday was writing this in his *Diary of a Tour*: 'The city of St
Andrews is only a shadow of what it has been. The streets
show grass as well as pavement.' Again Thomas Pennant, the
naturalist and traveller, noted in his *Tour of Scotland* of 1772:
'St Andrews. . . .numerous towers and spires give it an air of
vast magnificence . . . but so grass-grown, and such a dreary
solitude lay before us, that it formed the perfect idea of
having been laid waste by pestilence.'

The eighteenth century's two most distinguished visitors
were Daniel Defoe (*circa* 1660−1731), the pamphleteer and
Whig confidential agent and promoter of the Union, who
averred in his *A Tour through the Whole Island of Great Britain*
(1724−6): 'The city of St Andrew is, notwithstanding its many
disasters . . . a handsome city . . .' − and, Samuel Johnson

(1709—84), who, accompanied by James Boswell (1740—95), called at the town while on their tour of the Hebrides. They arrived after 'a dreary drive in a dusky night' on Wednesday, 18 August 1773, and put up at 5 South Street, then known as 'Glass's Inn' (and so it remained until around 1830). After a good supper they visited St Leonard's College, preceded by their landlord, Andrew Glass, carrying a candle and a waiter a lantern.

Next day the curious couple were introduced to Professor Robert Watson who had bought St Leonard's, by their erstwhile travelling companion from Leith, the advocate William Nairne (later Lord Dunsinane) and breakfasted in their company. They visited the cathedral, St Rule's and the castle and had dinner with a college of professors led by James Murison, rector of the university. They next saw Holy Trinity church and looked at St Salvator's College and after tea they supped at Professor Watson's and met the great-granddaughter of the murdered Archbishop Sharp.

On 20 August they breakfasted with Professor Andrew Shaw and visited the garden and grotto owned by the Hon. Lt. Col. John Nairne, then tenant of Queen Mary's House. The grotto was made out of the ruined portico on the north side of St Leonard's chapel, and herein were displays of skulls, a 'wonderful large lobster claw', and relics of the cathedral tracery and vaulting. In the garden they viewed 'a fine old plane tree' concerning which Col. Nairn averred that there was only one more 'large tree in the county'. This allowed Johnson to score a sarcastic point: 'A tree might be a show in Scotland as a horse is in Venice'.

The travelling pair left St Andrews at noon of the same day and in his *Journey to the Western Isles of Scotland* (1774) Johnson wrote: 'St Andrews seems to be a place eminently adapted to study and education, being situated in a populous, yet cheap country, and exposing the minds and manners of young men neither to the levity and dissoluteness of a capital city, nor to the gross luxury of a town of commerce, places naturally unpropitious to learning; in one the desire of

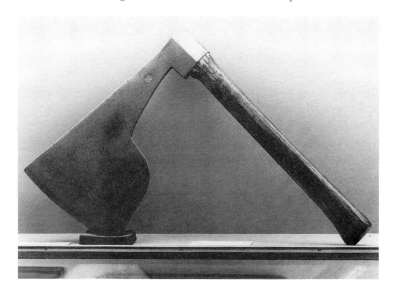

The Headsman's Axe of the burgh of St Andrews, now part of the small display at the Town Hall in Queens Gardens. It bears the initials H.C. in punched design. In 1622 an execution in St Andrews cost £17.12s.0d Scots, or £1.46p in modern sterling.

knowledge easily gives way to the love of pleasure, and in the other, is in danger of yielding to the love of money.'

In 1806 Robert Forsyth, in his *The Beauties of Scotland* wrote this: '. . . the magnitude and apparent grandeur of the buildings are evidently disproportioned to any business or active employment here carried on; and the town has the appearance of being too great for its present inhabitants, and of falling into ruin from the want of present wealth or energy.'

And Sir Walter Scott (1771−1832) was able to reflect in his *Diary* on his two visits to St Andrews, the first in 1793, and the second in 1827 when visiting Charleton. In 1793 he had gone up St Rule's tower and had carved the name of his then love, Williamina Belsches, on the turf beside the castle gate. In June 1827 he visited the burgh with the Blair Adam Club (some nine or ten members met every summer at the Kinross home of the Lord Chief Commissioner William Adam, from 1816 to 1832) which had made a visit to the East Neuk; and Sir Walter made this reflection as recorded by his son-in-law John Gibson Lockhart in *Life of Sir Walter Scott*: 'I sate down on a gravestone, and recollected the first visit I made to St Andrews, now thirty-four years ago. What changes in my feelings and my fortunes have since then taken place! — some for the better, many for the worse. I remembered the name I then carved in runic characters on the turf beside the castle-gate, and I asked why it should still agitate my heart. But my friends came down from the tower, and the foolish idea was chased away.' In his novel *The Pirate* (1830), Scott has his character, young Triptolemus Yellowley, study at St Andrews, with the 'rector of St Leonard's' as his cicerone.

St Andrews was to rest on the vestiges of its former greatness to about the beginning of Victoria's reign, but from the 1750s were planted the seeds of the burgh's future as a centre of advanced education, a holiday resort and a mecca of golf. Families were beginning to come to St Andrews more regularly for summer sojourns, and polite society paced the foreshores, some soberly, some more eccentrically like Lady Buchan who held elegant, if bizarre, tea-parties in St Rule's cave. It was a place to return to retire to like Adam Ferguson (1728–1816), the philosopher and alumnus who bought an estate nearby.

By Sir Walter Scott's death in 1832, St Andrews was changing and expanding and the greatest number of fundamental changes were to be carried out by the ruthless Major Playfair, who was to become Provost Sir Hugh Lyon Playfair (1786–1861), and Hon Custodian of Crown Property in the City. Playfair had retired from active military service in 1834 and, taking up residence at St Leonard's, began to pursue a local political career. Once on the Town Council he set about harmonising the various warring factions on the council and retrieved the burgh funds that had been dissipated. With military precision he undertook a survey of the burgh to see what needed to be done.

The first task was to lay footpaving along the whole length of South Street from the Pends to the West Port, and an alignment of the buildings on the street (the lime trees were added 1879—80). Street lighting was improved to make St Andrews one of the best lit places in Britain. Improvements were made to the Scores, Lade Braes, the Harbour and the burial ground, and Playfair Terrace, constructed in 1846, was named after the major. None of this was easily accomplished; Playfair encountered much vested interest and lethargy, but with diplomacy and bullying he was able to set the tone for the development of modern St Andrews. In recent years scholars have opined that Playfair's work has been overplayed and a more significant part was played in the development of modern St Andrews by Dr John Adamson (1810—70), who as Medical Officer of Health completely overhauled the burgh's sanitary arrangements.

The arc of land set around the outer limits of the burgh developed in its own way and from the twelfth century the territories were confirmed on the priory by Papal Bull. We hear of a fortalice at Kinkell pre-1591; the Grange was a priory farmstead and Priest Den Parks recalls the ecclesiastical landlords. The Kinness Burn was spanned at the Shore Bridge of *circa* 1789, set by Robert Balfour's House, and was forded at Greenside Place (a new bridge was built here in 1931) as was the Swilken Burn. The ford across the Kinness Burn at Bridge Street gave way in time to 'Maggie Murray's Bridge' at the foot of Melbourne Brae. Maggie Murray was the daughter of William Murray landowner at the Bassaguard (Bess Acre) from 1767 and of the land at Wal Wynde ('Well Wynd' — Melbourne Place and Bridge Street), and had married Andrew Wallace, shipmaster. Maggie built the bridge at her own expense and in time the Murray properties hereabouts were purchased by William Gibson of Dunloch who built the Gibson Hospital and City Park.

A dozen or so mills are mentioned as being in Fife by the twelfth century, of which three are noted for the St Andrews area. The mill at Kilrimont is likely to have developed as the later Abbey Mill (the Sanatorium of St Leonard's School of 1899 is on the site of the Abbey Mill and Brewhouse) which seems to have been disused as such by 1861; Putekin (Peekie) Mill was granted to the priory in 1144; and Nidie Mill on the Eden ceased to work in the late nineteenth century. In *circa* 1240 Cairnsmill was given to the priory and Denbrae Mill was built by Prior Hepburn in the 1480s. Probably all of these mills were quite small and were driven by a paddle-wheel. They were places of social intercourse for the townsfolk. The most famous of all St Andrews' mills was Lawmill which belonged to the priory, and was probably founded in the thirteenth century although we only have a sure record of it by the sixteenth century. By 1660 the mill was owned by the burgh, and by this time it had the unusual feature of double grinding stones; after 1848 it was back in private hands. Four other mills were known within the burgh: New Mill — the Plash Mill — may be dated at least to 1550 when it was feued by the priory; it was bought by the town in 1696 and changed hands once or twice until 1866 when it was sold to the proprietor of New Park; it ceased to function as a mill after that. Craig Mill was built by Prior Hepburn after 1483 and seems to have been in ruins by 1606. Shore Mill was built in 1518 by the Prior and in 1558 fell into private hands, then burgh ownership; in the late 1890s it was sold to the gas company. The Windmill is mentioned by 1598 by the Cow Wynd (cf: modern Windmill Road), and it was probably erected as a tower mill in the 1580s on the site of an earlier mill, and might have been one of those 'ready made' mills that were imported from Ghent at this time.

To the west of the town lie the lands of Strathtyrum and here stood, before 1400, the Strathtyrum Cross. After the Reformation, Strathtyrum estate was resumed by the Crown and conferred on the family of the Duke of Lennox. By 1596 the estate had passed to James Wood of Lambieletham and was later assumed by the Inglises who sold it to Archbishop James Sharp in 1669. Soon after this the estate was subdivided and in 1782 Strathtyrum was acquired by James Cheape and the Cheape family still own the property.

Strathtyrum House dates from 1720−40 and is a three-storey building with a southeast section of 1805−15, stables of 1817 and a mausoleum of 1781. Strathtyrum Lodge dates from 1821 and the gates are early eighteenth century.

CHAPTER 6

Folk of the Fisher Cross and Harbour

Sea fishing was an important part of St Andrews' economy from long before the Middle Ages, but after the loss of a small fleet of five yawls and a dozen fishermen during the storm of 4 November 1765, the fishing trade almost entirely ended. Until the end of the century the town was supplied with fish from the East Neuk ports until in 1803 two Shetland yawls, with a six-man crew each, began to ply from St Andrews. The first local motor-powered fishing vessel to be used at St Andrews was the deep-sea herring boat *Theodosia,* owned by Will and John Cross of 1911.

The nearest fishing havens to St Andrews harbour were at Boarhills and Kinkell — where there was a now vanished castle and chapel set where archaeologists have found Pictish refuse middens — and here the boats tied up when rough weather kept them out of the harbour. St Andrews' harbour walls were rebuilt in 1654 with stones from the castle and the quay was rebuilt and the harbour was widened and deepened during 1845—46. Despite rapid silting St Andrews harbour was bustling during 1770—1925 with fishing boats and ships for exporting potatoes and grain, and the importation of coal, iron, paving stones and timber. A passenger packet-boat plied to Leith from 1830 to 1914. The development of the present harbour was largely due to the efforts of the philanthropist, poet and musician, George Bruce (1825—1904) who lived in Market Street. He was immortalised in his sponsorship of the Bruce Embankment. The pier at St Andrews was originally of wood, but this was destroyed by the storm of December 1655; thereafter a half-length pier was built with stone from the castle and regularly repaired. There was a lighthouse at the end of the 290 yard long pier until 1849, and a new beacon was placed beyond the pier to

A late Victorian scene showing some of the now vanished fisher houses at the east end of North Street. The medieval Fisher Cross was sited to the far left opposite No 52 North Street; it was removed *circa* 1800. On the site of the houses to the right was built the Rectory (1938) of All Saints Episcopal Church and the modern university residence of Gannochy House (1971) (*St Andrews Preservation Trust*).

85

replace a decayed oak one on Lady's Craig Rock. The cross pier was built in 1722 and was damaged by the storm of 1727 and rebuilt; it was repaired in 1938. The East Bents (with its putting green of 1925) was regularly breached it seems by the Kinness Burn, and a protective wall was erected here in 1877. The inner harbour dates from 1785—89 and was crossed by the Shore Bridge (just beyond Balfour House) of *circa* 1789 — in the thirteenth century this bridge was known as Stermolind ('Mill Bar') and Bow Bridge by 1655; the footbridge linking The Shorehead and the East Bents dates from 1927. It should be remembered too, though, that St Andrews harbour was not the town's most ancient seaport. Large schooners and sloops still sailed up the Eden well into the Victorian era to the anchorage at Guardbridge; this was the quay for the sawmill and the Seggie distillery and for agricultural products. The port, known as the 'Water of Eden', was the main harbour of the Metropolitan See.

The Shorehead of St Andrews was formerly the site of two taverns and a malthouse, and fishermen's stores; it developed as a tenement, with the name of *The Royal George* and was condemned as a slum in 1935. The site was redeveloped with flats and houses during 1965—66. Behind *The Royal George*, at East Kirkhill, lies the old signal station and the remains of a fifteenth century doorway of the old Provost's Manse. It is interesting to note that most of the burgh's working people lived in overcrowded tenements which were given names of ships of the line, like *Great Eastern, Great Western* and *The Pembroke.* Although fisher families did live at the harbour edge, the main *quartier* was in the shadow of the cathedral's northwest aspect.

A large number of St Andrews families gained a livelihood from the open sea-fishing, netting locally for ten months, then off the Caithness coast for the other two. St Andrews' old fisher quarter was set within that area of land contained by North Castle Street, South Castle Street, Gregory Lane (once Dickieman's Wynd, or Foundry Lane), Gregory Place and the East Scores. The fisher folk had their own school in

A delightful two-storey house at No 19 North Street with its forestair, the only example of such a pillared stairway in St Andrews. The house at Ladyhead, in the heart of the old fisher quarter, was renovated in 1949, and abuts Marine Place which was built by the Sea Box Society. This benevolent society was founded in 1643 and continued until 1921.

Gregory Place by 1847 (on the site of the old Salvation Army citadel) which moved further east in 1856 to become the East Infants' School. Gregory Lane was the site of a fishermen's reading room and social club set up in 1907, of which the main donor was the Scottish Coast Mission; a former reading room for fishermen was sponsored by Captain Cox of the coastguard and Dr A. K. Lindesay, and the new one was opened by Major W. Anstruther-Gray MP. Marine Place was built by the old charity of 1643 known as the Sea Box Society (ended 1921), abutting the Ladyhead, which street led to Gregory's Green (sited in front of the war memorial of 1922) named after Professor David Gregory (1712–66). The focal point of the fisher community was their own Cross (sited opposite 52 North Street) known as the 'Little Cross', which was removed around 1800. This cross was repaired *circa* 1616 and there was probably a fish market in the vicinity although the bulk of St Andrews fish was sold at the Buttermarket. At one time fish could only be sold at these markets; transgressors were fined (from £1 to £10 in 1800) and were incarcerated in the tolbooth until such fines and court expenses were paid. In those days the street level of North Street was somewhere between three and five feet below the present level. Regularly townsfolk of St Andrews complained that the fisherfolk used North Street for the deposit of stinking fish guts and as a depot for their gear. Several of the fisherfolk and seafarers worshipped in Holy Trinity church where a 'Sailor's Loft' was sited until 1789.

Many of the fisher families, like the Gourlays, the Wilsons and the Chisholms, still have descendants in the town. As the fishing industry declined in the burgh, some of the fishermen became golf caddies and retained their blue jerseys and peak caps. Several of the old fish sellers walked as far as ten to fifteen miles radius of the town each day to sell their fish. One great personality in the town was the fish-seller Mrs Henry Clark, known locally as 'Joan'. She wore the distinctive costume of the traditional Scottish fishwife of white stockings, elastic-sided boots, a striped skirt over a multitude of brightly

Students on the ritual walk to St Andrews pier after attending service at the university chapel. The 290-yard long pier was originally of wood and in its first form was demolished by the storm of 1655. A shorter pier was built in 1656 using stone from the castle, but it was repeatedly damaged by tide and weather. A long concrete extension was erected in 1898, and until 1849 the pier had a succession of lighthouses (*Peter Adamson*).

The Shore and Harbour, St Andrews, looking towards the houses and flats of 1965–66, built on the site of one of the old tenements known as the 'Royal George'. To the left stood the Shore Mill of *circa* 1518, reconstructed in the seventeenth century and in 1964–66. The footbridge across the largely 1845–46 rebuilt medieval harbour was opened in 1925, leading to the putting green of the East Bents.

coloured petticoats, a red-knitted jacket, a red shawl and fisher apron. Joan's spotless house, from which she issued to sell flounders, white fish and cod from her wheelbarrow, was at 11 South Castle Street. She was working hard up to ten months before her death on 4 September 1927 aged 75.

The fisherfolk were a very superstitious group; they did not like seeing a clergyman before they set sail, for instance, and they evolved a taboo language in which such words as pig, orange and storm were never used in conversation lest back luck ensue. Because many of them had the same surname nicknames were very common among the fisherfolk.

For years the fisherfolk claimed the right to collect the mussel-scalps on the Eden estuary which they used for bait, and those scalps formed one of the town's oldest and most remarkable industries. The fishermen had long claimed them as a free perk, but ultimately they were charged so much per basket by the Town Council who had been granted a monopoly in early charters. This led to a continual argybargy between the fishermen and the authorities. The fishing trade had so declined by the 1940s that the scalp foraging died out because of labour and transport costs.

During the Seven Years War, 1756—63, the Press Gangs were active in St Andrews. Originally the Pressmen were employed to force paupers, vagabonds and criminals into the army and navy; but in time of war they were unscrupulous recruiters of those who had seamanship skills. It seems that in the years 1759—60, three naval Press Gang lieutenants were active in the town; these lieutenants, Fowler, Betson and Bruce, got friendly with the fishing population with a view to recruitment. Alcohol was a common bribe and when the recruits were well-oiled they were shanghaied by the 12-man Press Gang. Although the Provost of the time, James Lumisdaine of Rennyhill, and the magistrates complained, it had no effect, although there are no records of the numbers of recruits 'taken' by the Press Gangs in the town.

George Bruce in his *Wrecks of St Andrews Bay* averred that St Andrews' first lifeboat was acquired about 1801 as a consequence of the wrecking in 1800 of the sloop the *Janet* out of Macduff, Banffshire. And for around 138 years the burgh retained its own lifeboat; the era ended in 1938 when, because of the decline of the fishing industry, it was difficult to recruit skilful volunteers. The last lifeboat was the twenty five feet self-righting Rubie-type *John and Sarah Hadfield* which had been put into commission in 1910. The vessel was sold to Valvona of Portobello to be used as a pleasure cruiser. The Life Guard Corps of the Step Rock Amateur Swimming Club launched their patrol cutter (the first in Scotland) in 1938 to enhance safe bathing.

CHAPTER 7

The Rise, Fall and Rise of the University

St Andrews has been a seat of learning since the days of the Culdees in whose cloisters the *ferleggin* (man of letters) had charge of the manuscripts and the ruling and teaching of a school. The running conflict between the Culdees and the Augustinians about who had the superior right to do what, included the education of novices (the early students), and it was not until around 1211 that Archdeacon Laurence the Ferlinn was allocated funds for teaching within the priory of St Andrews. It is likely that the Culdees continued a teaching rôle under the Augustinians until the formers' total absorption. The motivation for Scotland to have her own university came about through politics and war. Although Scots scholars continued to study at Oxford and Cambridge, after the Wars of Independence, the increasing troubles with England, and the Great Schism in the Papacy from 1378, wherein England supported a Pope who was not acceptable to the Scots and their allies, drove Scottish students to seek their advanced education elsewhere.

The origins of the university of St Andrews came in three well-defined steps. The need for establishing advanced education was brought into focus by the diocese of St Andrews' senior clergy under the leadership of Bishop Henry Wardlaw, with the support of King James I (still a prisoner in England), Prior James Bisset and Archdeacon Thomas Stewart. Abbot Walter Bower tells us in the *Scotichronicon* that after the Feast of Pentecost, 11 May 1410, a *Studium Generale Universitatis* was founded; this meant that teaching began on this date with the main objectives of advancing learning and maintaining the Catholic faith. At this point the 'university' was a voluntary society of teaching clergy who were chartered on 28 February 1412 in the chapter house of

The western elevation of St Mary's College, founded in 1537 on the site of the Pedagogy of 1430, itself abutting the now vanished Church of St John the Evangelist, the first building to be erected for the emergent university. Left to right the Stair Tower dates from 1552, the Frater Hall and Principal's House from 1544. In the foreground stands the sundial of 1664 and at the foot of the Stair Tower is Queen Mary's Thorn, reputed to have been planted (or its predecessor) by the queen in 1565.

the priory, by Bishop Wardlaw. This was an important step as the intent of the charter was to bring about a working and amicable understanding between the burgh and the new university teachers. Wardlaw made it easy for the two to flourish together and the teachers were under the protection of the bishop in terms of their liberty and privileges and now the teachers were able to buy their needs in the burgh without tax.

Bower tells us of the first teachers who were all educated in France, and most at Paris. Within the faculty of Canon Law were: Laurence of Lindores, who expounded the fourth book of *Sentences* (opinions) of the scholastic theologian and philosopher Peter Lombard; Richard de Cornell, Archdeacon of Lothian; John Litster, Canon of the Priory of St Andrews; John de Schevez, Official of St Andrews; and William Stephen, later Bishop of Dunblane. In the faculty of Philosophy and Logic were: John Gill, sometime clerk of the diocese; William de Foulis, priest of the diocese of Dunblane; and William Croser, priest of the diocese of St Andrews.

Bishop Wardlaw's charter, then, just gave the school protection, but it could not confer degrees, neither was it recognised in Christendom as having any 'university status'; only these important things could be granted by one of the two heads of Christendom, the Pope or the Holy Roman Emperor. So far as Scotland was concerned the only lawful pope was Peter de Luna, Cardinal of St Mary in Cosmedia, who ruled as Antipope Benedict XIII, from his stronghold of Pensicola in the diocese of Tortosa, Aragon, Spain. So an approach was made to Benedict in the name of the infant school, its promotors the Church of St Andrews, the King of Scots and the Estates, all of whom formed the sovereign authorities of Scotland. As a consequence six papal *bulla* were issued on 28 August 1413, the Feast of Saint Augustine of Hippo, which formulated the small school as an equal with the great schools of Europe. It thus became a *studium generale* in Canon and Civil Law, Theology, Arts, Medicine and 'other lawful faculties'. It now had the power to examine candidates for doctorates and masterships and to present such candidates to the diocesan bishops for *ubique docendi*, the license which meant that they could teach anywhere in Christendom. The Papal Bulls were brought to St Andrews by Henry de Ogilvy, priest of the diocese of St Andrews, and they arrived in St Andrews on the Morrow of the Purification of Our Lady, Candlemas, February 1414 after a long and arduous journey by land and sea from Spain.

Amid pealing bells the Bulls were welcomed by the townsfolk, and next day, they were formally presented to Bishop Henry Wardlaw in the refectory of the priory. Once the Bulls had been promulgated, the diocesan clergy and the

The 1846 cloisters within the Quad of St Salvator's College; soaring above is the tower of the college founded by Bishop James Kennedy in 1450. The collegiate chapel was built 1450—60 and the spire was added to the tower *circa* 1550. The chapel contains the 1460 tomb of the founder and the vestry to the left was added in 1930.

canons processed into the cathedral church, singing the *Te Deum*. At the High Altar, Alexander Waghorn, Bishop of Ross, intoned the versicle and the collect *De Spiritu Sancto* (Of the Holy Ghost): *Deus, qui corda fidelium Sancti Spiritus illustratione docuisti: da nobis in eodem Spiritu recta sapere; et de ejus semper consolatione gaudere.* (God, who didst teach the faithful by sending the light of the Holy Spirit into their hearts, grant that, by the gift of that Spirit, right judgement may be ours, and that we may ever find joy in his comfort). The day was spent in feasting with bonfires in the streets at night. On 6 February, the celebration of the Coming of St Andrew's Relics, the rejoicing was continued; this day Prior James Bisset celebrated Mass with prayers for the infant university and the Bishop of Ross preached the sermon.

Within the new university there was little distinction between professors and students, as there is today; all were scholars in the pursuit of learning within an academic society. The head of this society was the Rector, elected by the *Comitia*, all the people who had been legally 'incorporated' or matriculated in the university and who formed the general congregation.

The first Rector of the university, the *Acta Facultatis Artium Universitatis Sanctiandree 1413–1588* tells us, was the theologian philosopher Laurence of Lindores (*circa* 1372–1437), Inquisitor of Heretical Pravity in Scotland, who introduced the system that all of the members of the university were divided into four 'Nations' (*Albania*-Fife; *Angusia*-Angus; *Laudonia*-Lothian; and *Britannia* – the diocese of Glasgow and Galloway, replaced by *Fifa* by the sixteenth century), according to their place of birth. Each of these Nations had its Procurator, and a proxy (Intrant) for voting. In medieval times the Rector was elected the first Monday of March after which a meal of wine and fruit was supplied at the Rector's expense.

The early rôle of the Rector was to preside over the university's general congregations, supervise its order and discipline and embody in his person the 'corporate authority'

Time and weather have sculpted this strange design in the form of a face on a stone in the front wall of the tower of St Salvator's. The pious believed that the face was that of the martyr Patrick Hamilton etched into the stone by the psychic power of his martyrdom as he was burned at the stake below. Today the story of his martyrdom is told on a plaque set into the wall by the gate at the foot of the tower; it reads: 'The initials on the pavement nearby mark the spot where Patrick Hamilton, member of the university, was burned at the stake on 29 Feb 1528, at the age of 24. On the Continent he had been greatly influenced by Martin Luther, and on his return to St Andrews he began to teach Lutheran doctrines. Having been tried and found guilty of heresy, he was condemned to death, thus becoming the first martyr of the Scottish Reformation' (*Peter Adamson*).

of the university. He also instituted proceedings over debtors to the university, aided the students with their commitments to the university and was the main link-man between the university and the burgesses. In his work the Rector was assisted by a number of assessors, generally nominated by the Nations. After 1475 the students were excluded from the election of Rector, and while the vote was restored in 1625, the actual choice of Rector was limited to the heads of the colleges, and after 1642, to the Professors of Divinity. No significant alterations took place until 1858, when the system was changed and from that date the Rector no longer represented the 'corporate identity' of the university, and instead of being elected annually he was elected for three years.

After 1862 a certain party political flavour entered the election of Rector with the nomination of F. Maule-Ramsay, Marquis of Dalhousie, Palmerston's erstwhile Secretary of State for War, and Sir William Stirling-Maxwell, the Conservative MP (Stirling-Maxwell won); this flavour continued until 1892. Over the years some Rectors have been outstanding in their work for students and for the university, others, like the Marquis of Dufferin and Ava, have been, to say the least, uninterested, while others again like the 3rd Marquess of Bute (often called the 'First Working Rector') have been generous benefactors, popular with students, while being a thorn in the flesh of Principals (in Bute's case he did not often see eye to eye with Principal Donaldson).

Today the rôle of the Rector (defined by the Act of 1858) is as 'ordinary President' of the University Court, and general spokesman of the students both inside and outside the university, and he is chosen by the students themselves. The Rector consults the Students' Representative Council — instituted 1885 and one of the two component organisations of the students' association — as to students' needs and problems. The Rector appoints an Assessor who sits on the University Court. The university has had many famous people serving as Rector, from the English philospher and

The collegiate church of St Salvator, known as the University Chapel, was renovated in 1861−62 and 1929−31, and its most distinctive feature today is the tomb (1460) of the college's founder Bishop James Kennedy. The chapel contains the much altered 'John Knox pulpit'. In 1594, and many years after, the Commissary Court met in the chapel, as did Cromwell's judiciary to dispense justice, and from 1759 to 1904 the parishioners of St Leonard's worshipped until their new church was erected at Rathelpie (*Peter Adamson*).

member of Bentham's utilitarian school, John Stuart Mill who served 1865–68, to the Scottish author and dramatist Sir James Matthew Barrie who was Rector 1919–22. In recent years the students have gone more for 'media' men and women like John Cleese, Frank Muir and Tim Brooke-Taylor, and in 1982 elected the first female Rector in journalist Katharine Whitehorn.

The superior of the Rector in medieval times was the Chancellor, and from 1413 to 1689 the office was held (with three brief intervals) by the bishops and archbishops of the (arch)diocese. When the system of episcopacy was abolished the Chancellor was thereafter appointed by the *Senatus Academicus*, who combined the rôle until 1858 when the prerogative was invested in the General Council. The actual duties of the Chancellor have always been vague, but this comment is to be found in the *St Andrews University Calendar* (1983–84): 'The office of Chancellor has existed since the foundation of the University and no comprehensive definition of its powers has been made in any modern statute. The most authoritative definition is contained in the return made by the University to the Commissioners of 1826 which states: "The Chancellor is head of the University. He is consulted on all, public matters relative to its welfare, and he is also Conservator of its privileges. The power of conferring degrees is vested in him . . ." The Act of 1858 provides that the Chancellor is to be elected by the General Council and to hold office for life. He is the ordinary President of the General Council and must give his sanction to all "improvements in the internal arrangements of the University" proposed by the University Court. He appoints an Assessor on the Court'. Since 1697 the office of Chancellor has been held mostly by aristocrats, with a career soldier (Field Marshal Earl Haig of Bemersyde, 1922–28), a Prime Minister (Earl Baldwin of Bewdly, 1929–47) and an academic.

The *University Calendar* goes on to define the rôle of the Vice-Chancellor: 'From an early date in the history of the

Deans Court, built *circa* 1570 on the site of the Archdeacon's lodgings of the medieval archdiocese of St Andrews. Altered 1864–5 and 1950–1, it is now a postgraduate residence. It retains its vaulted understorey and draw well; above the entrance gateway are the arms of Sir George Douglas (d.1606), who renovated the medieval property, and in front of the gates the martyr Walter Myln was burned in 1558.

University it was customary for the Chancellor to appoint a Vice-Chancellor to confer degrees in his absence. The Act of 1858 explicitly empowers the Chancellor to appoint a Vice-Chancellor who may in his absence discharge his office "in so far as regards conferring degrees but in no other respect". By a convention uniformly observed since 1859 the Principal of the University is appointed Vice-Chancellor.'

When the university began, its teaching and ceremonial were conducted where the lecturers lived, but for important 'congregations' and faculty meetings they met in the refectory of the priory. Tradition has it that from an early date the university acquired some interest in a group of buildings in South Street known to scholars as the Chapel and College of St John the Evangelist. Here we find the Faculty of Arts meeting in 1416, and three years after they seem to have been in possession of the property. In January 1419 Canon Robert of Montrose, Rector of the Church of Cults and Chaplain of Honour of the Apostolic See, gave a tenement of land on the south side of South Street 'to found a College of Theologians and Artists' all confirmed in honour of 'Almighty God, to the Blessed Virgin Mary, and especially to the Blessed John the Evangelist and All Saints'. This property was vested in Laurence of Lindores, first 'Master, Rector and Governor of the said college'. The site of the first building of the university today is the western end of the Parliament Hall, South Street, and we know that in medieval times the 'College of St John' was a long double tenement incorporating a chapel and a small chantry college. The Feast of St John the Divine, Apostle and Evangelist, author of the Fourth Gospel, was the main official festival of the college, and was held on 27 December when the Master would say the Collect *Ecclesiam tuam, Domine, benignus illustra* while the most senior clergymen present would intone the Mass of St John. The next building developed for the university came with the founding in 1430 of a *Paedagogium* by Bishop Wardlaw on a site just west of the College of St John, which was replaced by the founding of St Mary's College in 1537.

In medieval times the age of entry to the university was thirteen and each student conformed to a seniority system, with the *bejaunus* being the youngest, rising to *bachelor* after third year (with *semi-bachelor* as an intermediate stage) and *magistrand* in final year. Eventually the term *bejant* applied to first year students, *semi* for second year, *tertian* (*bachelor* in

The north and east elevations of St Salvator's College. Lower College Hall and the North Wing date from 1846, and the East Wing from 1829—31 with an extension of 1906. Behind the East Wing are the Purdie Chemistry laboratories (1905), attached to a main building of 1892. On the cliff above the sea lie Edgecliffe (1864—66) and Kirnan (1866), while away to the right is seen St Salvator's Hall (1930) with its extension of 1940 (*Peter Adamson*).

the nineteenth century) for third year, and *magistrand* for fourth. The scarlet gown still worn by students at St Andrews is considered to be a post-Reformation tradition, but the custom of 'Raisin Monday' probably goes back to the earliest days of the university. By tradition each *bejant* (female *bejantine*) acquires a 'Senior Man' or 'Senior Woman' from the third or fourth year to whom they can turn for assistance in their first year; these 'academic parents' introduce them to friends and into the university social circles. In this way first year students are rapidly introduced into academic life. During the first term (Martinmas) the honoured custom of 'Raisin Monday' is held in which *bejants* and *bejantines* present their academic parents with a pound of raisins (now usually in the form of a bottle of wine) in exchange for a ribald receipt in Latin. The whole carnival atmosphere, which expects the *bejants* to dress up in outrageous costumes, is a unique feature of St Andrews student life.

Before the end of the Middle Ages the society of scholars at St Andrews had formed themselves into three endowed colleges, St Salvator's (1450), St Leonard's (1512) and St Mary's (1537). In 1747 the colleges of St Salvator and St Leonard were united into a single United College and have so remained to modern times, although St Leonard's College was revived as a non-statutory college to encourage and support research students and care for postgraduate students.

The College of St Salvator was founded as a consequence of the university going through a bad patch in the mid-fifteenth century. With the expulsion of the English scholars from Paris in 1436, Scottish students renewed their traditional gravitation to France and denuded the university's potential intake. This, combined with inter-college squabbling at St John's and the Pedagogy, led to a decline in the university's funds and influence, and the whole needed a new focus. To this end the asthmatic Bishop James Kennedy (*circa* 1408–65) founded a new college dedicated to the Holy Saviour on 27 August 1450 in North Street. The college remains on the same site today and its dedication to St Salvator comes from the English rendering of the Scots *Sanct Salvatour*. Kennedy's foundation was confirmed by the Bull of Pope Nicholas V in February 1451, and reconfirmed in an updated charter by Pius II in 1458.

Today the college founded to teach Theology and Arts with a faculty of thirteen persons to symbolise Our Lord and His Apostles, and funded by teinds from the parishes of Cults, Kemback, Dunino and Kilmany, remains one of the most noteworthy assemblages of architecture in Scotland. It was the first real academic college in Scotland and its charter

The Younger Graduation Hall of the University of 1923—29, donated by Dr & Mrs James Younger of Mount Melville, and opened in 1929 by the then Duchess of York, now HM Queen Elizabeth the Queen Mother. Its building was a part of the significant renovations at the University during this period, which included the Collegiate Chapel of St Salvator and the old Parliament Hall in South Street.

says that its members were 'to live together in a collegiate manner, and to eat and sleep within the bounds of the college'. The original buildings of the college were arranged round a cloister court, with the upper stories being used as living quarters and the ground floor as lecture rooms. Only the frontage of the medieval buildings remains, but the college formerly had a hall against the wall of the south end of Butt's Wynd, a walled garden to the back leading to the riggs of Stanycroft next to the Swallowgait; in front of the chapel, and now under the roadway of North Street was the collegiate church cemetery. The cloister court was demolished in 1763. What can be seen today is Lower College Hall of 1846, the East Wing of 1831 (with extension of 1906) and the Cloister building of 1846 set around The Quad. The gateway now set outside the college chapel in North Street probably came from the cloister buildings of Kennedy's time.

The tower of Bishop Kennedy's college remains as a landmark in the town and dates from the 1450s; the original spire of timber and lead was erected by Archbishop James Beaton around 1530, and it was destroyed during the great siege of the castle of 1546—47, whereupon the tower was used as a gun emplacement to attack the castle — the present spire was added by Archbishop Hamilton around 1550 and its parapet was added in 1846. The tower archway (giving access to the old college court and the modern Quad) is surmounted by a panel showing Kennedy's arms, flanked by niches for now vanished statues; these would probably be of religious figures hacked down at the Reformation. The coat of arms of Bishop Kennedy, surmounted by its mitre, is to be found on various parts of the college and the college arms themselves were only officially matriculated in 1949 and depict an orb surmounted by a Latin cross. In the belfry hangs the great bell of the college traditionally called 'Katherine' and the tower would probably have a clock in medieval times. The bell called 'Katherine' measures two feet seven inches in diameter across the mouth and bears the inscription:

SANCTVS. IAC[*OBUS*]. KENNEDUS. EPISCOPUS. S[*ANC*]
TI. ANDRAE. AC. FUNDATOR. COLLEGII. S[*ANC*]TI.
SALVATORIS. ME. FECIT. FIERI. ANNO. 1460. KATH-
ARINAM. NOMINANDO. D[*OCTOR*]. JAC[*OBUS*].
MARTINUS. EIUSDEM. COLLEGII. PRAEPOSITUS. ME.
REFECIT. A.D. 1609. ET. D[*OCTOR*]. ALEX [*ANDE*]R.
SKENE. EIUSDEM. COLLEGII. PRAEPOSTIUS [*sic*]. ME.
TERTIO. FIERI. FECIT: JOHN. MEIKLE. ME. FECIT.
EDINBWRCH. ANNO. 1686. ET DOCTOR JACOBUS
COLQUHOUN IRVINE, EQ.[*UES*]. EJUSDEM COLLEGII
PRAEPOSITUS ME QUARTO FIERI FECIT ANNO 1940.
For: 'That holy man, James Kennedy, Bishop of St Andrews
and founder of the College of the Holy Saviour, had me cast
in the year 1460, giving me the name of Katherine. Dr James
Martine, Provost of the same college, re-cast me in the year
of our Lord 1609; and Dr Alexander Skene, Provost of the
same college had me cast a third time: John Meikle cast me
at Edinburgh in the year 1686; and Dr James Colquhoun
Irvine, Knight, Principal of the same college, had me cast a
fourth time in the year 1940'.

'Katherine' is accompanied by the old bell of St Leonard's
College called 'Elizabeth' cast at Ghent around 1512, to be re-
cast in 1724 and 1940; 'Elizabeth', a very unusual name for a
bell, was brought to St Salvator's when the steeple of St
Leonard's College was demolished in 1764. Standing one
foot six inches in diameter across the mouth 'Elizabeth' is
inscribed: ME. ELIZABETHAM. LEONARDINAM.
ANTE. BIS. CENTVM. ANNOS. GANDAVI. FACTAM.
ET. TEMPORIS. INIVRIA. DILAPSAM. COLLEGE [*sic*]
LEONARDINI. IMPENSIS. REFECIT. ROBERTVS.
MAXWELL. ANNO. 1724. ED[*INBVRGI*]. ET ME BIS
CENTVM ANNIS ITERUM ELAPSIS IAM FRACTA
VOCE SENESCENTEM REFICIENDAM CURAVIT
JACOBUS COLQUHOUN IRVINE HUJUS COLLEGII
PRAEPOSITUS 1940. For: 'I am Elizabeth of St Leonard's;
cast at Ghent two hundred years before and impaired by the
ravages of time, Robert Maxwell re-cast me at Edinburgh in

the year 1724 at the charges of St Leonard's College; and after the passage of another two hundred years, when my voice had cracked and I was growing old, James Colquhoun Irvine, Principal of this college, took care to have me re-cast in 1940'.

At the foot of the tower, and set into the causeway, are the letters 'P.H.', the initials of one Patrick Hamilton, the meaning of which is now revealed for all to see on the plaque commissioned and donated by Professor Emeritus Jack Allen in 1988. The plaque reads: 'The initials on the pavement nearby mark the spot where Patrick Hamilton, member of the university, was burned at the stake on 22 February 1528, at the age of 24. On the Continent he had been greatly influenced by Martin Luther, and on his return to St Andrews he began to teach Lutheran doctrines. Having been tried and found guilty of heresy, he was condemned to death, thus becoming the first martyr of the Scottish Reformation'. If the visitor looks above the arms of Bishop Kennedy on the forefront of the tower he or she will see the weathered stone in the form of a 'face', which the pious declared was the image of Hamilton etched in stone by the psychic power of his martyrdom.

The chapel contained a number of tombstones but the main burial was of the founder. It is probable that Kennedy's tomb was designed for the cathedral, where one would expect the diocesan bishop to be buried, but some time between the consecration of the church in 1460 and Kennedy's death in 1465, a change of plan was carried out. The tomb is formed of a Gothic niche with a tomb-chest covered with a black marble slab; on this may have rested a now vanished effigy of the bishop destroyed by the Reformers. The stone is grey micaceous freestone, but the carving is of the Tournai school to Kennedy's own design with the theme of the Bringing of Good (Christianity) to a world of sin and death. The stone chapel roof was renovated in 1773, and this work destroyed much of the early decoration and maybe the tomb too; and considerable restoration took place in 1930, a stone screen

St Leonard's Chapel of *circa* 1405, extended 1512, abandoned 1761 and restored in 1910 and 1951. It is all that remains of a Culdee foundation acquired by the Augustinians in 1144 and known as the Hospital of St Leonard. This hospital was re-founded in 1512 by Archbishop Alexander Stewart and Prior John Hepburn. To the left is seen the massive Renaissance monument of Robert Stewart, Earl of March, Commendator of the Priory and titular Bishop of Caithness; he died in 1586. The picture at the east end of the chapel is 'The Legend of St Leonard' by Walter Pritchard (1956) (*Peter Adamson*).

being erected at the west end of the nave and the famous 'John Knox' pulpit replacing an earlier one. At the time Kennedy's tomb was opened, and not for the first time, for in 1862 Kennedy's bones had been gathered and placed in an oak casket made by Charles Conacher, the St Andrews cabinet maker, for £3. 2s 7d (£3.13½p). By 1930 this casket was disintegrating and a new silver/bronze casket (supplied by Sir Henry Keith) replaced it to contain the bishop's bones. Incidentally James Kennedy had his own barge, *Salvator*, 'the biggest that had been seen to sail upon the Ocean', which, with the tomb, had cost him a great deal of money; the vessel was wrecked off Bamburgh, Northumberland, in 1473.

Something of the beauty of the medieval embellishments of the church may be seen in the celebrated mace of St Salvator's college. The mace was ordered for the college by Bishop Kennedy in 1461, and has a hexagonal open shrine as its head with the Holy Saviour as a main emblem. Angels show the symbols of the Passion (a cross, a scourging-pillar, a spear) and the shields of St Andrews, Bishop Kennedy and St Salvator's College are displayed along with the figures of a king, a bishop and a Franciscan friar (or, maybe a merchant). This inscription appears on the base of the mace: 'Johne Maiel (*Jean Mayelle*) Gouldsmithe and Verlette off Chamer til the Lord the Delfyne has made this Masse in the Toun of Paris the yher of our Lorde mcccclvi.' A silver-gilt medal (attached to the rod of the mace by a chain) says: AVISEES A LA FIN JACOBVS KANEDI ILLVSTRIS SAN[C]TI ANDREE ANTISTES AC FV[N]DATOR COLLEGII S[ANCT]I SALVATORIS CVI ME DONAVIT ME FECIT FIERE PARI[S]IIS AN[N]O D[OMI]NI MCCCCLX. For: '*Avise la fin* — the French equivalent of the Latin *Respice finem*, 'Consider the end' — James Kennedy the illustrious bishop of St Andrews and founder of the College of St Salvator, to which he gifted me, had me made at Paris in the year of the Lord 1460.' The mace shows that it was repaired several times, particularly in 1685.

The University Observatory (1940) comprises five modern buildings, and is set within its own parkland. The University has been associated with astronomy since the days of James Gregory who held the Regius Chair of Mathematics there from 1668—74; he is widely regarded as the 'father' of the reflecting telescope. His observatory has now vanished (it was on a site near the foot of Westburn Wynd) but his determination of the 'meridian line' is remembered in an inlay on the upper floor above Parliament Hall.

The university owns other maces, the Mace of the Faculty of Arts, commissioned 1414—15 and completed 1418—19, and the Mace of Canon Law made pre-1457. There are also two modern maces, that of the School of Medicine of 1949 and the University Mace of 1958.

At the Reformation the church's medieval religious services came to an end, although the educational functions of the college continued in part and it was reduced to a Protestant dominated Arts college. The church was stripped of its 'papist' furnishings and it stood empty and desolate, and was ultimately used, along with its vestry, as a meeting place for the new university Commissary Court, although we are told that it was 'occasionally used for preaching' in the late sixteenth century. In 1747 United College was formed of the colleges of St Salvator and St Leonard and from 1759 to 1904 the parishioners of St Leonard's parish worshipped in the church. The University entered a full occupancy of the chapel as a 'university chapel' in 1904.

Perhaps the most famous St Salvator's graduate was James Graham (1612–50), who succeeded his father in 1626 as Marquess of Montrose. A signatory of the National Covenant in 1638, Montrose's signature is still extant in the Matriculation Register of the University; he was at St Salvator's during 1627–29.

With the decline of the Pedagogy, the sixteenth century opened for the university with financial and recruiting problems, and these were confronted by the young Archbishop Alexander Stewart; in the event he was to die with his father the king at Flodden in 1513. Alexander had studied under Erasmus's tutelage and was a scholar of note. Events developed so that an ancient hospital adjoining the church dedicated to the sixth century Gaulish abbot St Leonard became available – this had been an institution that had belonged to the Culdees and had been given to the Augustinians in 1144 by Bishop Robert, and which had subsequently been turned into an almshouse for old women; the old women were expelled for being neither spiritual nor worthy. On 20 August 1512 a charter proclaimed the conversion of the hospital – once a haven for pilgrims to the Shrine of St Andrew – and church of St Leonard into 'the College of Poor Clerks of the Church of St Andrews'; confirmed by James IV in 1513, the college became known as the 'College of St Leonards' and was largely founded by the work of Prior John Hepburn, and initial accommodation was found for the library and tutorial rooms at the priory. At first a master (a canon of the priory), four chaplains and twenty poor scholars (effectively Augustinian novices) made up the college which was run on monastic lines with football

Journalist Katharine Whitehorn, the university's first woman Rector, 1983, and Rector's Assessor, Paul Chennell, are 'dragged' by students past the 14th-century Pends gateway, on her first tour of the town. The position of Rector dates back to the University's inception in 1410, and has been filled by many prominent people in British public life (*Peter Adamson*).

(and such 'dishonest games') being forbidden and no woman was allowed within the college precincts, except a laundress who had to be at least fifty years of age and inordinately plain. The college was to last through the vicissitudes of the Reformation and Episcopacy until in 1747 it was united with St Salvator's and its buildings were sold as private residences. For instance, Samuel Johnson's host, Dr Robert Watson, was one of the residents.

Today the site of St Leonard's College is incorporated in St Leonard's private school, but there is public access to the college chapel from The Pends. St Leonard's College was revived in the 1980s as a non-statutory college to care for post graduate students, and encourage and support research activities. The oldest part of the chapel seen today is the nave and west portion of the choir which dates from *circa* 1144; the rest of the chapel is Romanesque; the buildings were extended eastwards, *circa* 1544–50, to include a now vanished western tower and south porch. It functioned as a parish kirk after 1578 and remained so until abandonment in 1761, whereafter the church became ruined. In 1853 the interior of the church was cleaned out and the windows unblocked; and in 1910 the University Court renovated the building, re-roofed it and re-glazed the windows, but nothing further was done on the church until the extensive renovation in 1948–52.

The chapel contains an early piscina – probably taken from the cathedral – and several interesting monuments including a much worn one thought to be that of the college founder John Hepburn. Prior Hepburn's body was exhumed in the 1840s, under the supervision of Professor Gillespie, and the cadaver was found to be in a shroud and enclosed in lead, but with no coffin. Also exhumed were Robert Stewart, Duke of Lennox, Bishop-elect of Caithness whose Renaissance type mural monument is set against the east end of the north wall. His epitaph reads:

IN[*P*] ORTV FLVCTVSQVE OMNES CLASSEMQVE REL-

The 'beardless bejant' Martin Davidson, in his rôle as Kate Kennedy, awaits departure in 1976 for a tour of the town with 'her' uncle Bishop James Kennedy (played by Martin B. Passmore) in the Quad of St Salvator's College. The St Andrews University Kate Kennedy Club is a society which organises various charity events and promotes the colourful 'KK' procession each spring depicting characters from the history of Town and Gown (*Peter Adamson*).

INQVO ME SPECTANS MVNDVMQVE OMNEM PASCE-
SQVE R[*ELI*] NQVE.
('Safe in harbour I put behind me the ocean and my fleet. Beholding me, put behind you the whole world and your burdens.')
Exhumed at the same time was James Wynram, sub-prior and after 1560, Superintendent of Fife, who died at the age of 90. His epitaph says:
1582 MVLTA/CVM DE/AMBVLAVERIS DEMVM RE/ DEVNDVM/EST HAC
CONDITIONE (*IN*)/TRAVI V[*T*]/EXIREM.

('Long as your pilgrimage has been, you must return at last.
I came on condition that I should depart.')

St Mary's College was founded on 12 February 1537 by
Archbishop James Beaton, and was designed on the advice
of French masons working at Falkland Palace. The college
was completed 1543—44 and was based on the existing 1430
Pedagogy to teach Theology, Law, Physic and other 'liberal
disciplines', all 'under the invocation of the Assumption of
the Blessed Virgin Mary'. Archbishop Beaton's probable
intention in his foundation was to promote the teaching and
recruitment of well-educated secular clergy for his archdiocese. When the archbishop died in 1539 the continuation
of the college scheme was carried out by his nephew Cardinal
David Beaton, but the buildings were completed by
Archbishop John Hamilton *circa* 1553—54. The original
buildings were set around a four-sided court, of which only
the much altered north and west blocks remain; the Common
Hall of the college stood to the south and the college chapel
to the east.

Today St Mary's — where Divinity is taught — is one of
the most attractive locations in St Andrews. Its entrance is in
South Street and the visitor passes through an archway into a
quad. The distinctive iron gateway bears the motto *In
Principio Erat Verbum* ('In the beginning was the Word': *St
John's Gospel*, 1.1.) and the coat of arms incorporates devices
of Archbishop James Beaton and Archbishop James
Hamilton, with the *fleur de lis* representing the original
dedication to the Blessed Mary of the Assumption. To the
west the quad is bounded by the Principal's House (1544),
the Frater Hall (1544) and the Stair Tower (1552), outside of
which is the thorn tree whose predecessor is deemed to have
been planted by Mary, Queen of Scots in 1565. The belfry is
the home of fan tailed pigeons from around the late 1880s.
On the South Street exterior wall of the Principal's House is
the Royal Coat of Arms with *In Defens anno domini 1613*. The
north range of St Mary's incorporates Parliament Hall and
Library, bearing on the South Street side the arms of former

Andrew Carnegie (1835—1919), industrialist and philanthropist, who was Rector of the University 1901—7. Carnegie's gifts to the University included a new organ for the University chapel, the recreation park and pavilion (1904), a gymnasium (1905), and an extension to the then University Library (1908).

Chancellors of the university while the south side displays a fourteenth century emblem of the passion from the earlier church on the site dedicated to St John the Evangelist. Parliament Hall gains its name from the fact that the Scottish parliament sat at St Andrews from 26 November 1645 to 4 February 1646 at which 6/- (30p) for lodgings were paid per night for the gentry and 4/6d (22½p) per servant. The south range of St Mary's incorporates the Reading Room of 1890 and the Carnegie Library of 1908. In the middle of the quad is the evergreen holm oak (*quercus ilex*) of *circa* 1750. Nearby is the offshoot of the Glastonbury Thorn (from the Benedictine Abbey of Glastonbury, Somerset, itself mooted to have been planted by St Joseph of Arimathea) planted to commemorate the Moderatorship in 1949—50 of Principal G. S. Duncan. The old University Library has been converted for use by the Department of Psychology. South of the quad now lie the Bell-Pettigrew and Bute buildings for the study of Botany, Zoology, Anatomy and Physiology and the new Department of Botany is sited on the Old Botanical Garden area.

In truth the constitution of the university has developed steadily since 1410 and its substance is not set out in any one document. Its traditions and customs have been prescribed by the enfolding Universities (Scotland) Acts 1858—1966. The University Court is the supreme governing body of the university, in which all of the university's revenue and property are vested. The Court is made up, and prescribed by statute, of around twenty people drawn from the university and outside bodies. Its ultimate responsibility is for the maintenance of properties, management of residences, appointment of staff, finance and business management. The *Senatus Academicus* holds autonomous authority in matters academic, which elects six members of the Court. It is made up of the principal, the professors and certain other members of the university *ex officio*, and elected non-professorial staff and four students. The office of Principal of the University,

Sir James Irvine (1877–1952), Principal and Vice-Chancellor of the University of St Andrews 1921–52, with Stanley Baldwin, Chancellor of the University 1929–47; Baldwin was Prime Minister of the National government during his chancellorship. Known as 'Jimmy the Princ' to generations of students, Irvine served through a period which witnessed the largest expansion of the University since the Middle Ages (*University of St Andrews*).

incidentally, dates from 1858, although it was only created as such in 1953. The academic structure of the university is made up of three Faculties — Arts, Divinity and Science (with Medical Sciences).

The Students' Union, a social centre of student life, is

E

situated in St Mary's Place on the site of the old West Park Hotel. The Union developed from the provision of a Common Room or Reading Room for students in the chapel cloister, *circa* 1864, but a scheme for a more substantial Union was set afoot in 1885. As funds grew temporary quarters were found in the old Imperial Hotel (now the Argyle Hotel, North Street), but a move to Butt's Wynd was made in 1892; a coffee shop and meeting place is still to be found in the Old Union. The old building was in fact the much altered fifteenth-sixteenth century residence of a former *alumnus*, 'the Admirable' James Crichton of Eliock; his descendant, the 3rd Marquess of Bute, bought the house for the Union and paid for its restoration. An eastern reconstruction was carried out in 1923. A Women's Students' Union was established in the early 1900s and a permanent home for them was subscribed by Mrs Andrew Carnegie of Skibo in the western half of the North Street Union. The two unions were amalgamated in 1963—64 and the coat of arms (incorporating the arms of Low of Blebo and Crichton-Stuart of Falkland, principal benefactors) granted to the Men's Union in 1949 was adopted by the new amalgamated union under their motto *Stat Scotia, Stat Aula* ('Stands Scotland, Stands this House').

Today students either live in one of the Halls of Residence or in private accommodation. To date there are ten Halls of Residence, the oldest being the University Hall of Residence for Women Students (University Hall for short) opened in 1896, four years after women students first appeared at the university. University Hall has expanded to include the neighbouring mansion of Westerlee of 1865—67 and is incorporated in the annex of Wardlaw Hall Residence. This Hall caters for women students only and the two residences solely for males are St Salvator's Hall (with Gannochy House) and Hepburn Hall. When it was opened in 1930, St Salvator's Residence ('Sally's') was the most up-to-date in Europe; Hepburn Hall, opened in 1947, was named after Prior Hepburn, founder of St Leonard's College, and Gannochy opened in 1971. All the other Halls are 'mixed sex': John Burnet Hall (1965), formerly the Atholl Hotel (*circa* 1890—1900) was donated by Captain H. K. Salvesen of the Salvesen Shipping Co and was named after Professor John Burnet the noted Greek scholar; Andrew Melville Hall (1968), North Haugh, takes its name from the founder of Scottish Presbyterianism; David Russell Hall (1971), Wester Langlands, Buchanan Gardens, is named after Sir David Russell, a former Chancellor's Assessor and university benefactor; Deans Court (1951) was opened as an annex to St Salvator's Hall in 1931, and is set apart as a residence for postgraduate students; McIntosh Hall (1930) was the gift of Emeritus Professor William C. McIntosh (1838—1931) and was formed around his basic bequest of his house, 'Chattan House', 2 Abbotsford Crescent. The whole has extended to include the entire sweep of Abbotsford Crescent from the basic reconstruction of 1939. Two other residences have interesting 'background stories'. Hamilton Hall (1949), with Eden Court, was once the Grand Hotel (1895) and is named after Archbishop Hamilton and the House of Hamilton. During the 1930s this hotel was the venue of 'royal' visits by blue-bloods and celebrated golfers and was used by the Air Ministry during World War II. In 1948 a proposal was mooted to sell the hotel to the Roman Catholic Bishops of Scotland as a teachers' training college; but this caused a furore amongst the local Presbyterians and the bishops' offer was rejected and the university bought the building. St Regulus Hall (1944) adjoins the gardens of St Mary's College and is set at the foot of Queens Gardens. Formerly the building was the first home of the St Andrews School for Girls Co (later St Leonard's School), then it became the St Regulus Hotel and the building was bought from the Younger Estate in the 1920s. This hotel, incidentally, was favoured by Their Royal Highnesses Princess Helena Victoria (1870—1948) and Marie Louise (1872—1957) — the daughters of HRH Princess Helena, daughter of Queen Victoria — who took a suite here in 1886; they caused much local stir and attended services at Holy Trinity. Staff houses are also located at Albany Park, Fife Park, Angus House (off St Mary's Place) with Stanley Smith House.

No mention of the student presence in St Andrews would be complete without a comment on the Kate Kennedy Pageant of late Spring. This very colourful costume pageant appears to have originated in 1849 as an end-of-term frolic by final-year Arts students. It takes its name, tradition has it, from the supposed christian name of Bishop James Kennedy's niece, one Kate Kennedy, who the speculators of history further add, also gave her name to the tower bell at St Salvator's. In reality, of course, it is more likely that the bell was named after St Catherine of Alexandria, the martyr famed for the 'Catherine Wheel' of bonfire night and whose feast was celebrated on 25 November in medieval times. Whatever is the truth it seems that at the 1849 frolic one student dressed up as 'Kate' and capered at the centre of the noisy masquerade which, in time, spilled out into the streets of St Andrews. When the frolic became more boisterous the professors tried to ban it and this suppression made it a symbol of undergraduate freedom. By the 1860s Kate Kennedy Pageant had become a procession through the streets and in time the students' high spirits on this day brought them into conflict with the local authorities and the whole thing was banned in 1874; this ban remained almost total until 1926. The pageant is organised by the Kate Kennedy Club which was founded in 1926 by Donald Kennedy and James Doak, two students who had been inspired by the rectorial address on 'Courage' by Sir James Barrie the Rector. In his address Barrie had mused aloud as to the historical figures associated with the university he would have liked to meet, and Kennedy and Doak saw the revival of the procession as the nearest thing to Barrie's idea. Today some sixty to seventy characters take part from St Andrew himself to Field-Marshal Earl Haig, and new characters are added from time to time. Traditionally Kate

Jack Nicklaus, regarded by some as the greatest golfer of them all, receives his honorary degree in the University's Younger Hall (*Peter Adamson*).

Kennedy is played by a male student, and 'she' rides in a carriage with her uncle the bishop who is dressed in full canonicals. The procession comes out of the university Quad and proceeds down North Street to the castle, via the Scores. Then, by way of Market Street, the West Port and the cathedral it returns to the Quad. It was a happy day for St Andrews when Kennedy and Doak persuaded the then principal, Sir James Irvine, to lift the nineteenth century ban on the procession, as the Kate Kennedy Pageant is one of Europe's most vibrant events. Today the stated aims of the Kate Kennedy Club (which remains an all-male organisation) are to 'preserve traditions, to raise money for charity and to foster town-gown relationships'.

From its beginning in the fifteenth century, and throughout the sixteenth century, St Andrews university educated most of the leading figures in church and state in Scotland, and after 1659 it became the focus of the new national scheme of education grounded in the parish schools which arose out of the Reformation. Although its life was continually interrupted by the political troubles of the sixteenth and seventeenth centuries the university retained its academic influence in the education system in Scotland. Following the Act of Union of 1707, though, and the earlier abolition of Episcopacy, the political and economic shift to Edinburgh and Glasgow greatly affected the university and the town and during the eighteenth century the university went through a period of acute depression. During 1826–30, however, the university was subject to a searching investigation by a Royal Commission and this gave the impetus for the supplying of new buildings and changes in constitution, and under such principals as Sir David Brewster and Sir James Donaldson the university was given a new lease of life and, thus refreshed, it entered the twentieth century with a new strength and reputation which was further enhanced by Sir James Irvine and Sir Thomas Knox who between them spanned the years 1921–66 as succeeding principals. The affiliation of the University College of Dundee in 1881 to 'make it form part of the University of St Andrews' was effected in 1897 and in 1898 the Conjoint School of Medicine was established at Dundee. The foundation of the University of Dundee in 1967 brought all these arrangements to an end and today the university is again wholly in the town of its birth.

CHAPTER 8

The Town Churches and Their Stories

As well as the cathedral, the church of St Mary of the Rock and the hospital and college chapels, there were other medieval churches and two further important religious houses in St Andrews, namely the foundations of the Dominicans (Blackfriars) and the Franciscans (Greyfriars).

The Order of St Dominic of Friars Preachers was founded at Toulouse in 1215 by St Dominic (1170–1221) of Caleryega who was anxious to promote the skilful defence of the Catholic faith against heresy and the better instruction of the people in the principles of the Catholic faith and piety. The background of the Dominicans was an order founded on traditionally monastic lines living a contemplative life linked with an emphasis on the study of theology, but free from priestly or pastoral work and with a mobility to become itinerant preachers. As teachers the Dominicans first introduced a systematic course of education in Scotland. They took a vow of poverty and were therefore a mendicant order. They received their name of Blackfriars from their distinctive garb of white robe, scapular and cowl, and black open mantle with cowl. The Blackfriars are recorded in the *Chronica de Mailros* as having come to Scotland in 1230, a fact confirmed by the *Scotichronicon,* which says that they were encouraged to do so by Alexander II. It is Archbishop Spottiswoode, however, who says that they were brought to Scotland by Bishop William de Malvoisin of St Andrews, led by Friar Clement, and a house was founded for them in what was to become South Street, in 1274, by Bishop William Wishart. The actual date of the foundation is confused and is a matter of historical controversy, but the house did survive and was restored in 1516 by a legacy from Bishop

Elphinstone's estate and in 1519 the Dominican priories of St Katherine at Cupar and St Monan at St Monans, and the Hospital of St Nicholas were all united with the St Andrews house. It is known too that over the period 1464—1516, Blackfriars was not only restored in fabric but as a place for a study of sacred literature; and Dominican scholars were funded within the university. Up to 1481 when their own province was founded, the St Andrews Blackfriars were ruled by the English province chapter of the visitation of York whose local representative called every four years. In 1547 Blackfriars was burned by Norman Lesley and destroyed by the Reformers in 1559 when Knox preached in the burgh; and in 1567 Mary Stewart granted the properties of the Blackfriars to the provost, magistrates and council and community of St Andrews.

Today all that remains of the house of the Blackfriars, dedicated to the Assumption and Coronation of the Blessed Virgin Mary, is the *circa* 1525 three-sided north transept of their chapel; the boss in the vaulted roof bears the Emblems of the Passion and the fragment of building remains the only example of its type in Scotland. The conventual buildings lay under the present site of Madras School, and it is known that some of the medieval buildings were incorporated in Dr Young's school of 1622, demolished in 1833. The western part of the friary known as the 'Old Palace' was used as a dwelling until the early nineteenth century, and the remaining medieval religious site was handed over to the Board of Works in 1911. The house of the St Andrews Blackfriars was some twenty five feet wide (with length unknown) and probably had a square, spireless tower with cloister to the south with a central well; a garden probably ran down in tofts to the Lade Braes. Possibly there was a prior's house with outbuildings as well as a chapter house, sacristy and frater abutting the cloisters. Of the tombs within the chapel it is probable that all of the priors were buried in the aisle, and Sir James Balfour averred that Cardinal David Beaton was buried in Blackfriars in 1547. The Blackfriars cemetery was to the north side of the remaining transept and is now under South Street.

When the mendicant Order of Friars (Franciscans), founded by St Francis of Assissi (*circa* 1181–1226), came to Scotland is a matter of dispute, but King James IV declared that his grandmother, Mary of Guelders, had introduced the Observant Friars of St Francis in the mid-fifteenth century. Whatever the truth we know that the Franciscans were founded in their house at the corner of modern Greyfriars Garden and Market Street by Bishop James Kennedy in 1458, with a grant for a large house being gifted later by St Andrews' first archbishop, Patrick Graham, in 1478. These grants were confirmed by the charter of James IV in 1479. The St Andrews house of the Franciscans was colonised by Greyfriars from Edinburgh.

The extent of the property of the Greyfriars (the name by which the Franciscans were best known in St Andrews) may be set out by a line drawn from Woolworths, Market Street, to the site of the Northgait (opposite numbers 144–146 North Street), with a parallel line from the site of the Marketgait to Murray Place carpark. A fragment of the eastern wall of the friary runs behind modern Greyfriars Garden, and a fine arched gateway was removed from the North Street entry to the friary in the eighteenth century. The forty eight foot friary well was in the garden of 4 Greyfriars Garden (rediscovered in 1839, and cleaned out in 1886 when the parapet and iron guard were fitted) and the chapel was on the garden site of 1 Greyfriars Garden.

Greyfriars cemetery was discovered when work was being done on the nearby houses in 1904, and it was found to contain St Andrews burghers and their families buried in the chapel. The simple and unpretentious house of the Greyfriars was burned by Norman Lesley in 1547 and made over by its last Warden (Prior), Symon Maltman, to the St Andrews magistrates in May 1559, to be destroyed by the Reformers in June of the same year, but remained the

The remaining three-sided apse (1525) of the north transept of the church of the Blackfriars (Dominican) friary, South Street, set between 'weeping ashes' in the lawn fronting Madras College, itself founded by Dr Andrew Bell in 1832. Founded in 1274 by Bishop William Wishart, the Blackfriars precincts once incorporated Dr Young's Grammar School (1622) which was demolished in 1833.

property of the magistrates until the grounds were confirmed as being the property of the burgh by Mary Stewart in 1567. The two dozen or so Greyfriars at St Andrews acted as confessors to the students of St Salvator's College and influenced the spiritual life of the university within their rôle as evangelists rather than academics. Bound by vows of poverty, obedience and charity, the St Andrews Greyfriars went forth from the burgh to 'promote and fortify the Catholic faith, to strengthen the Christian religion and to sow the word of God more abundantly in the hearts of the faithful' in the major towns of Scotland. One of the most prominent of the St Andrews Greyfriars was Friar Robert Keith, a distinguished theologian who was the house's first Warden.

Two other now vanished medieval churches were to be found in St Andrews. One, 'St Peter's Overlooking the Sea', was situated at the junction of Gregory Lane and the East Scores; stones from the church were found in 1887 and 1927. Another church, the Chapel of the Holy Trinity, the Virgin and St Duthac, sited opposite to St Leonards Lane, was possibly founded by James III in 1487; but the building had gone by 1538. St Duthac (d.1065) was the Bishop of Ross, venerated for his miracles and prophecies, and had quite a following in the East Coast villages.

Two parishes are associated with modern St Andrews and its environs, the seaboard parish of St Andrews itself, taking in the old town, and the parish of St Leonards which was once made of four detached parts mostly surrounded by the parish of St Andrews. By an Order of the Boundary Commissioners of 1890 the two parishes were reconstituted in part, but the old St Leonards parish had its origins with the Hospital of St Leonard and the College of Poor Clerks of the Church of St Andrews (St Leonard's College). Within these parishes certain town churches were established that remain today.

The Scottish Episcopal Church has a strong showing in St Andrews within a sea of Presbyterianism. A province of the Anglican Communion, the Scottish Episcopal Church had survived the vicissitudes of the alternating religious climates from the Reformation to the seventeenth century, and was disestablished after the unfortunate audience between William Ross, Bishop of Edinburgh, and William III in 1688, when the bishop was considered to have snubbed the monarch. An Act of Parliament of 1689 established a Presbyterian Church of Scotland. There followed a period in which Episcopalians were harried, persecuted, impoverished and held in scorn. Although they were evicted from the establishment, many of the Episcopalian clergy and congregation took courage from the Act of Toleration of 1712. If they were prepared to accept the House of Hanover they were given freedom to worship, but many Episcopalians

A mid-Victorian photograph of North Street showing the now vanished Episcopal Church of 1825—70; the church was later removed, stone by stone, to Buckhaven. The University building called College Gate was built here in 1953, and the corner tower house abutting St Salvator's dates from *circa* 1540. To the right stood 'Beethoven Lodge' (*University of St Andrews*).

were Jacobites and brought their church into bad odour because of their support of James Edward Stuart in 1715 and 1745. The St Andrean Episcopalians had a perfectly legitimate 'meeting place', the Burgh Court Book of St Andrews tells us, in a house on the south side of South Street. Yet, after the Jacobite defeat at Culloden in 1746, local tradition has it that their altar table and furnishings were dragged out into South Street and burned. Nevertheless the St Andrean Episcopalians survived in secret and records of their activities are extant; some of these were found at the beginning of the nineteenth century in a tobacconist's shop, where portions of the pages had been used to wrap snuff. The documents showed that the Episcopalians were active in St Andrews during 1722—87. As time went by the religious climate improved and one of the first Episcopalian priests in St Andrews was the Rev David Lindsay who must have cut a dash in the burgh streets for he is mentioned by James Boswell in his *Journal of a Tour to the Hebrides,* under the date 19 August 1773: 'We saw in one of its streets a remarkable proof of liberal toleration: a nonjuring clergyman strutting about in his canonicals with a jolly countenance and a round belly, like a well-fed monk.'

The first modern Episcopal Church in St Andrews was sited in North Street; its foundation stone was laid on 27 August 1824 and its site abutted the modern university College Gate of 1953. Consecrated in 1825, and dedicated to St Andrew, the church survived until 1870 when it was shipped stone by stone aboard the *Sea King* to Buckhaven, having been bought by the Free Church for £130.

The Episcopal congregation was soon to have a new church, St Andrew's, Queens Terrace. Its foundation stone was laid on 31 July 1867, with full masonic honours, and the church was built to the plans of Sir Robert Rowand Anderson; dedicated in 1869, the church was consecrated in 1877. The tower of the church was erected in 1892, but demolished as unsafe in 1938.

By 1895 this six hundred-seat church was proving too small for the burgeoning congregation which included many 'poor fisherfolk'. So, in 1903 a mission church was established for the fisherfolk in North Castle Street; soon the house adjoining the site, known as Castle Wynd House, was bought for the Priest-in-Charge. In 1907 the dedication stone was laid for a stone chancel and by 1909 a bell tower was added to the church long called the 'bundle kirk' because of the parcels handed out to the needy. After World War I moves were set in motion by Mrs Annie Younger, the wife of Dr James Younger of Mount Melville, to complete the church in stone and additional land was acquired around the site; the fisherfolk who lived in houses on this land were rehoused in Saint Gregory's building set on the site of an old foundry. The church now acquired a nave, chapel and baptistry with

St James's Roman Catholic Church, West Scores. The church was consecrated on 2 August 1910 and is the work of the architect R. F. J. Fairlie (1883–1952), and replaced the 'tin tabernacle' which had been erected in 1884 for the Roman Catholic congregation. The church's stained glass was made at Pluscarden Priory, near Elgin, in the 1960s.

subsidiary buildings, and a rectory was completed in 1939. Mrs Younger's provisions for the church were lavish from vestments to font, and all buildings and endowments were in memory of her daughter and son-in-law. The old Guide Hall with its gymnasium above has been converted into a bookshop and tearoom taking the title of the old fisher-quarter of Ladyhead. The courtyard of the church is particularly fine, dominated by the crucifix of the war memorial of Forest of Dean stone; this memorial was unveiled by Field-Marshall Earl Haig of Bemersyde in 1924. Inside the church is a fine carving of the Madonna and Child by Hew Lorimer which was set to the south of the nave as a memorial to Mrs Younger who died in 1942. Another memorial also catches the visitor's eye; the ship model hanging by the northwest part of the nave was presented in memory of the novelist Hugh Walpole (1884—1941) by his sister Dr Dorothea Walpole in 1954. The Lady chapel, with its dark green panelling of marble and alabaster altar, is movingly outstanding.

The congregation of Hope Park Church, City Road, had its roots in 1733 as a consequence of the Great Secession, itself the forerunner of the Disruption of 1843 which splintered the Presbyterian Church. These events were concerned with the preservation of freedom to worship God without dictation or financial support of an 'establishment', and spoke of the fierce independence of the Presbyterians who in 1559 split from the Church of Rome. The forefathers of Hope Park Church began worship at a prayer meeting at Balone Den, near St Andrews in 1738 and this emergent congregation first made up the Associate Congregation 1738—47 to become the 'Burgher Kirk' in St Andrews. One of their early meeting places during 1749—74 was at the pantiled house, a former barn, at Imrie's Close, 136 South Street; next they moved to Burgher's Close, 141 South Street, where they worshipped until 1827 when they moved to a chapel on the site of what is now 52 North Street as the

Holy Trinity Church at the junction of Logie's Lane, Church Square and South Street. In the background is the old city hall (now the public library) which had been built as the English School in 1811. The church tower is the only remaining part of the church that was built here in 1412.

United Presbyterian Church. By now the Associate Congregation had passed through the phase of being the General Association of 1747–1820 when the 'Burghers' and 'Anti-Burghers' united to form the United Secession Congregation. These were the days when to be seen inebriated in public drew a personal denunciation from the pulpit. The United Presbyterian Congregation was formed in 1847 when the United Secession and the Relief Churches united. By 1865 the United Presbyterian congregation had moved to Hope Park Church and by 1929 the United Free Church congregation was formed out of the United Presbyterian and the Free Church congregations. Thereafter Hope Park reverted to the Church of Scotland. The present church was built in 1864 and the church hall was opened in 1900.

Martyrs' Church was born out of the Disruption of 1843, and was formed out of an Association in connection with the Free Church, and one of the founding members was Sir David Brewster, Principal of the United Colleges of the university 1838–59, himself a staunch supporter of the Free Church movement. At first regular services began in the Secession Church (now Hope Park), but the first church for the congregation was opened in November 1843 on the site of the present church in North Street. A spire and new frontage were added in 1851 and the first manse was built in Kennedy Gardens during 1856–57 (a new manse was built in Irvine Crescent in 1967). In 1883 it was decided to introduce hymns as well as the psalms for the services and this engendered much protest particularly from the local historian Dr David Hay Fleming who 'denounced the innovation' from his pew on the day of their introduction. Hay Fleming carried on his protest 'by standing at the prayers and sitting at the singing of the psalms'; his protests were intensified at the introduction of instrumental music (which preceded the purchase of an organ in the early 1900s). The church was renovated in 1887.

At the union of the Free and United Presbyterian Churches in 1900, the church took the name of Martyrs' United Free

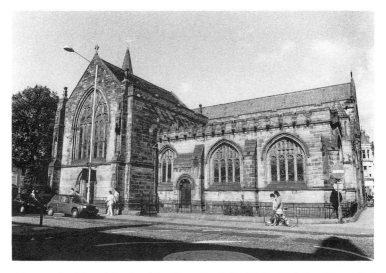

The south side of the Parish Church of the Holy Trinity. Founded on this site (a previous parish church of 1140 had been sited to the east of the cathedral) in 1412, the church as seen today was entirely reconstructed during 1907−9, the work of Peter MacGregor Chalmers (1859−1922). During 1430−1749 the church cemetery extended south into South Street.

Church, and by 1914 there was a movement to build a new church. The plans were thwarted by World War I, but in 1925 the scheme was revived. The church of 1843−44 was demolished in 1925 and the present church was opened in 1928, funded largely by the bequest of Henry Maitland of Balmungo. With the reunion of the United Free Church and the Church of Scotland in 1928, Martyrs' became the latter's charge. A church hall was added in 1934 and today the church contains a set of fine stained glass memorial windows.

From time to time town and gown have been at loggerheads and one celebrated occasion was when the *Fife News Almanac* of 1905 highlighted the 'St Leonard's Church Case'; which, according to the press, 'became notorious over the land'. The case arose from these historical circumstances: in 1903—04 the university authorities reclaimed the chapel of St Salvator's College for their own use. Now since 1759 the congregation of the dilapidated chapel of St Leonard's had been worshipping at St Salvator and were dispossessed by the university. Until the congregation acquired their new church at Rathelpie (in modern Donaldson Gardens) 'there was protracted litigation', said the papers of the day. The new church cost £5000 and was designed by the architect P. Macgregor Chalmers, in mock-Norman style, and was ready for worship by July 1904.

At the Reformation the clergy of the medieval church in St Andrews espoused the new faith, and the Church of Rome disappeared from Scotland. During the ensuing centuries the only Roman Catholic clergy to appear in Fife would be a few travellers and scholars, and hardly any Roman worship took place in St Andrews until after Pope Leo XIII (1810—1903) restored the Scottish Roman Catholic Hierarchy in 1878, although there were Roman Catholics identified in St Andrews by 1849 when the burgh was placed in the Cupar Mission. There seem to have been regular monthly Masses in St Andrews from around 1881, but there was no resident priest.

A scheme to build a Roman Catholic church in St Andrews was backed by James Robert Hope-Scott and it was on his land on The Scores that a Catholic Mission was planned and a temporary iron church was erected funded by the Marquess of Bute. The first priest, who was to become a St Andrews ecclesiastical personality, was Father George Angus (1842—1909), an Anglican turned Roman Catholic who first came to St Andrews during September 1884 and was housed at 22 Queens Street (now Queens Gardens — his house was on the site of a portion of St Regulus Hall); until the iron church was ready Father Angus conducted services in his home.

The iron church (known to the community as 'the Tin Tabernacle') was opened in 1885 and was dedicated to St James, Apostle and Martyr and cousin of Our Lord. A stone

The magnificent Dutch tomb of Archbishop James Sharp (1618–79), in the Sharp Aisle of Holy Trinity Church. Erected in 1681 by Sir William Sharp of Scotscraig — son of the murdered archbishop — the white and black marble monument shows a kneeling figure of the archbishop on the sarcophagus, while an angel holds out a martyr's crown.

presbytery for the priest was ready by 1886, next to the iron church. Curiously enough the excellence of Father Angus's extempore sermons brought a large non-Catholic congregation to his Sunday evening services, but all of his early Roman Catholic congregation were Irish.

Despite his popularity in certain quarters Father Angus had to endure hostility from some local Presbyterians nervous of anything Popish taking root in their burgh. Presbyterian rowdies demonstrated under his windows and the postmaster of the day objected to the use of 'Presbytery' in the address, proclaiming to all who would listen to his bigotry that the title belonged to the local Presbyterian clergy alone. Indeed it seems that some local folk broke into the Roman Catholic church and threw altar vessels into the sea. However, Father Angus was received as a friend at the tables of such local clergy as Dr. A. K. H. Boyd of Holy Trinity and the Baptist Minister and in due time he was made a member of the Royal & Ancient Golf Club.

In 1908 the St Andrews Roman Catholic Mission became a properly constituted parish taking in the area from the River Eden to Earlsferry and during 1909 — 10 the iron church was replaced by a stone edifice designed by the architect Reginald Fairlie funded by Mrs Annette Harmer of Canmore, The Scores. Her house was purchased in 1947 by the White Fathers as a study centre for their order; today it is the Roman Catholic chaplaincy for the university.

The present building of the Baptist Church, South Street, adjoining Rose Lane, was refronted 1901 — 02, but the original foundation of the congregation goes back to 1841 — 43. In those days the people who were to form the Baptist congregation worshipped at the Independent Church, which became the Congregational Church, itself established in Bell Street in 1856. The original Baptists formed a congregation in 1841 with their first meetings in the Old Town Hall; a Baptist Sunday School was established in 1844. Incidentally, a Christian Institute was functioning 1907 — 53 on the site of the old Post Office of 1892 in South Street, the present location of the Citizen Bookshop annexe. The Religious Society of Friends (Quakers), by the by, began regular worship as a group in St Andrews in 1964 and have met at various sites in the town. The Salvation Army began its work in the burgh in 1893, but closed down in 1904 to carry on once more during 1910—17. The work of the Army did not commence again until 1934. The Army had premises in Gregory Place (at the original fisher school at 1847), but moved into North Street in recent times.

Undoubtedly the most historical and ecclesiastically important parish church in St Andrews is Holy Trinity, South Street, colloquially dubbed 'the Town Kirk'. Dedicated to the Holy Trinity, a *circa* 1144 parish church stood at Kilrymont just to the south of the east gable of the cathedral, probably founded by Bishop Robert who had granted it to the Priory as a vicarage in 1165. The church received its formal dedication in 1243 by Bishop David de Bernham and was frequently utilised as a meeting place for the bishop's judiciary court and for some early university meetings. Probably stone from this old parish church was used by Prior Hepburn in the building of his walls. The twelfth century church was removed to the present site of Holy Trinity in 1410—12. Drastically altered in 1798—1800, the church we see today dates from the last reconstruction of 1907—9.

Those who wished the burgh to have its own parish church, within the town and away from the everyday influence of the cathedral chapter, were encouraged in their efforts by Bishop Henry Wardlaw; and in these works they were greatly assisted by Prior James Bissett, who had built the parish church of Cupar in 1415. The first vicar of the new parish church was William Bower, a canon of the Priory, who probably established the first manse (demolished 1882) for Holy Trinity in east North Street *circa* 1434. The site of the new parish church was on the lands of Sir William Lindsay, Lord of Byres, and Bishop Wardlaw gifted a neighbouring rig in 1430 to enlarge the cemetery which then took in most of the modern roadway in South Street beside the church and today's Church Square; in this graveyard was interred, in 1574, John Douglas, the first Protestant archbishop of St Andrews. The only surviving portions of the medieval building are parts of the west wall, some of the internal nave pillars and the tower (often used as the town jail), which today contains a change of seventeen bells (a memorial to Dr Playfair, minister of the First Charge of St Andrews 1899 – 1924, chief promoter of the restoration). The city Curfew is still rung from the tower every week evening at 8 p.m.

The bishop of the diocese was the superior of medieval Holy Trinity, and the rector of the church was the Prior of St Andrews who dealt with the church's financial and legal affairs; the vicar saw to the everyday running of the church assisted by a curate, both overseeing the duties of the master of works, who tended the fabric, while the parish clerk was the link man between the burgh and the clergy. In medieval times the parish clerk would be in holy orders and he sang the Mass, and cared for the church security and bells, and directed the secular clergy (sacristan, beadle) who rang the bells, attended to the church's more domestic arrangements and acted as doorkeeper.

Some thirty priests served the church, with its 33 altars, and twelve of their number acted as choristers, all under a procurator or hebdomador (second only to the vicar) for their order and discipline and to maintain the canonical services basically which, with some grouping, followed those of the cathedral. It was usual for the civic bodies of the town to maintain the altars within the parish church, while some were founded by individuals for the good of their immortal souls. When the church was built, the Holy Trinity Altar, for instance, was erected by the burghers in honour of Sir William Lindsay the founder, and the city magistrates and council were the patrons of the Altar of St Andrew. The devotion to the Holy Trinity — from the prayer *Gloria Patri, et Filio, et Spiritu Sancto* (Glory be to the Father, and to the

William Allan's depiction, engraved by H. Bourne, of the murder on Magus Muir, near Strathkinness, of James Sharp, Archbishop of St Andrews, on 3 May 1679. Once the minister of Crail, Sharp had turned his coat in his Covenanting enemies' eyes and was consecrated archbishop in 1661. Sharp is seen here being hacked to death in the presence of his daughter Isabel.

Son, and to the Holy Ghost) — was strong in medieval St Andrews, and the First Day of the Holy Trinity (the Sunday after Whitsunday), which had been established by St Thomas the Martyr of Canterbury in 1162, was one of pious devotion in the burgh calendar. The Altar of St Aubert, Bishop of Cambrai, was founded and maintained by the town's Bakers' Craft, or Guild, while the Altar of St Eloy of Limoges was maintained by the town's Hammermen.

In a walk around the parish church today it is worth noting the West Window (a gift of the Women of the Congregation, 1914), the memorial font to Dr A. K. H. Boyd, minister of the First Charge 1865—99, the Playfair (family) Aisle, the onyx, alabaster and Iona marble pulpit and the

John Knox Porch commemorating the Reformer. It was in Holy Trinity that Knox preached his infamous sermon on 11 June 1559 (on Our Lord's ejection of the buyers and sellers from the Temple) which incited the mob to unspeakable vandalism against the treasures and culture of the Medieval Church. The Sharp Aisle contains the white and black marble tomb and monument of Archbishop Sharp. James Sharp (1618−79), Archbishop of St Andrews, was a Royalist who went to England when the Covenanters abolished episcopal government in 1638. He came back in 1643, taught for a while at St Andrews University and became the minister of Crail in 1649. In due time his skill as a negotiator won him high praise and he was appointed Professor of Theology at St Andrews; as leader of the 'moderate party' he was chosen as Archbishop of St Andrews and consecrated in 1661. To those of fanatical Covenanting faith Sharp was now a turncoat and a 'government man' willing to agree to anything (even the Act of Supremacy of 1669 which gave the monarch complete authority in the church) to secure his position. An attempt was made on his life in 1668, but his enemies finally succeeded in his murder at Magus Muir, where he was dragged from his coach and stabbed to death on 3 May 1679.

The Sharp monument in Holy Trinity is of Dutch work and was erected in 1681 by Sir William Sharp of Scotscraig, the son of the slain archbishop. At Sharp's funeral on 16 May 1679, the sermon was preached by John Paterson, Bishop of Edinburgh, and Andrew Bruce, Bishop of Dunkeld, composed the following inscription . . . translated from the Latin.

'To the Lord God, supreme ruler of the world . This lofty tomb covers the unspeakably precious dust of the holiest of bishops, the sagest of state-councillors, the most saintly of martyrs, for here lies all that remains beneath the sun of the Most Reverend Father in Christ, James Sharp, Doctor of Divinity, Archbishop of St Andrews, Primate of all Scotland, etc., whom the University regarded, acknowledged and continually marvelled at as a professor of theology and philosophy, the Church as priest, teacher, and leader, Scotland as its Prime Minister, ecclesiastical and lay, Britain as the advocate of the restoration of His Most Gracious Majesty, Charles the Second, and of the monarchy, the world of Christianity as the man who re-established the order of Episcopacy in Scotland, good and faithful subjects as a model of piety, an angel of peace, an oracle of wisdom and a picture of dignity, enemies of God, the King, and the people as the bitterest foe of irreligion, treason and schism, and whom despite his character and eminence nine sworn assassins, inspired by fanatical rage, did with pistols, swords and daggers most foully massacre close to his metropolitan seat, under the noonday sun, with his beloved eldest daughter and his personal attendants bleeding, weeping and protesting, on May 3rd, 1679, in the sixty-first year of his age, piercing him with countless wounds when he had fallen on his knees to pray even for his murderers.'

When Sharp's tomb was opened in 1848 it was found to be empty of bones and relics. On the sarcophagus is a marble figure of the kneeling archbishop, and from a white marble cloud an angel holds out a martyr's crown. Behind the archbishop's head are the gold-painted words PRO MITRA, from which the Sharp family derive their crest and motto PRO MITRA CORONAM. A plaque below depicts the archbishop's martyrdom.

St Mary's Church, St Mary's Place, was erected in 1840 as extra accommodation for those who could not get into Holy Trinity. This church was demolished but the name remains as a location.

CHAPTER 9

At School and College

Two St Andrews schools receive the most public attention these days, Madras College and St Leonard's School, the latter being a public school for girls. Education, albeit with the sole intent of sifting out likely recruits for the church, was first developed in the town by the Priors of St Andrews, within their cloistered setting. All this came to an end at the Reformation and a Latin Grammar School developed in the town out of the turmoils of the religious upheavals. The Latin Grammar School, which was probably developed from *circa* 1570, was set on ground between the then ruined site of Blackfriars, South Street, and Lade Braes Lane (called Common Close by Regency times). The Grammar School served the town until another public school was founded *circa* 1755 on the site of the public library; this was the English School where no Latin was taught, but pupils were grounded in the '3Rs'. The English School was built largely at the expense of George Dempster of Dunichen, Provost 1760−61. These two schools were to form the basis of a new foundation.

Opened in 1833, 'The Madras College' was founded on the 'Madras', or 'Monitorial', system of education invented by the Rev. Dr Andrew Bell (1753−1832), Prebendary of Westminster Abbey and Master of Sherburn Hospital. A native of St Andrews — he was born in a house which stood on the site of 107 South Street (the modern Citizen Bookshop) — Bell was educated at the Latin Grammar School and entered the United College in 1769. After graduating he was employed as a tutor in Virginia, USA, and was ordained as a clerk in holy orders in the Church of England. In due course he embarked for India and became superintendent of the Madras Military Orphanage Asylum, India, a foundation

The Jacobean-style frontage of Madras College, South Street, opened in 1833 as a part of the educational foundation projects of Dr Andrew Bell (1753–1832). Built of Strathkinness stone, the College was the largest public building to be erected in St Andrews since the Reformation.

for the care and education of the orphans and Eurasian offspring of deceased British soldiers. Gradually Dr Bell evolved his Madras monitorial system of education (in which youthful members taught younger children) and returned to Britain in 1796 to become more involved in parish duties as a clergyman and as Master of Sherburn Hospital.

Long before the Madras College was opened, Andrew Bell had started to work on the idea of opening a school in St Andrews 'where the great body of the children of the place, rich and poor, may be educated under one roof'. Eventually plans were agreed upon and the Jacobean-frontaged school was begun with the foundation stone being laid on 9 April 1832.

Bell was not to live to see the opening of his school of Strathkinness stone built to William Burn's design as it rose to blend with Blackfriars, but the incomplete school was opened on 1 October 1833 to teach pupils at a full fee of 3/-

(15p) a quarter, with other pupils receiving free education. The first intake was the pupils of the English School and probably others from the private schools in the town. Children were to come from all over the UK to be taught at Madras, and they lodged with the masters or with people in the town. By 1834 the pupils of the old Latin Grammar School moved into Madras, and although it was a co-educational school from the first in spirit, few girls attended in the early years; a Lady Superintendent was not appointed until 1864, when girls then appeared in greater numbers. New buildings for Madras College, Kilrymont Road, were occupied by Madras pupils in 1967, and were officially opened in 1968.

A glance through the school's early records throws up a number of interesting facts. For instance, the appearance of the school — the largest public building to be erected in St Andrews since 1559 — did not please everyone. After his visit to St Andrews in 1844, the lawyer diarist and Lord of Session, Henry Thomas Cockburn (1779—1854), wrote: 'The thing called Madras College is at present a great blot. There should have been no commonplace, vulgar, bare-legged school there'. Early facilities at the school were spartan; privies were not added to the school until two years after it opened and it seems that Madras College always had a reputation for being cold despite ducted-air heating; one Rector 'Put on two sets of woollen underwear in October and *kept* them on till April'. Classes could begin as early as 6 a.m. and pupils were forbidden to bring firearms to school in 1836, and in the early days parents paid separate fees for each class, selecting the classes that their children should attend. The school was a prominent landowner in the town, purchasing the farms of Priorletham, Waterless and Pipelands in 1846 and Cairns in 1858; in this spirit Dr Edward Woodford, the classics master, kept a pig in the tiny yard behind his lodgings at Madras House East.

Madras College former pupils included Professor William McIntosh (See: McIntosh Hall) and Dr David Hay Fleming, mentioned many times in these pages. Two men were to carry on Dr Woodford's eccentricity. One was the colourful soldier-cum-writer Robert Marshall, who wrote the golf classic *The Haunted Major,* and the other was Martin Anderson (d.1932); Anderson was the artist who under the pseudonym of 'Cynicus' was celebrated for his satirical cartoons — he built his red-sandstone folly castle (demolished 1939) at Balmullo in 1903.

Writing in 1838, Dr James Grierson reported on the desirability of the then extant infants' school: 'So soon as the child can speak or walk, he may be subjected to a course of kind and interesting training under the management of an experienced lady in an infant school. Here exercise, music and elementary learning are beautifully mixed and alternated, that the infant of four or five years of age is far happier than if set free from all instruction and management whatever. All this may be obtained by every parent for a mere trifle. The infant school forms a proper nursery school for Madras College. There English reading and spelling are admirably taught so low as one shilling [5p] a quarter, whilst writing may be added for only three pence [1.5p] per quarter more.' He was talking of the infants' school — called Dr Bell's Infants School — sited behind the town church 1832—44. In 1844, at the cost of £800 the West Infants School was built in St Mary's Place and was hailed as 'a masterpiece of modern education'. Today the building is no longer used as a school but houses the town's registrar's office, and other local government departments. After the 1890 Education Act a Board School was established in Abbey Walk and continued as a part of 'comprehensive' education with Madras as a Junior High School until 1967.

Education in St Andrews was greatly reorganised by the passing of the Education (Scotland) Act, 1872, by which every parish and burgh had its elected School Board for the direction of education for children 'who might otherwise have grown up in ignorance and been nurtured in vice'. One of the immediate tasks of the School Boards was to 'regularise' the school system, build extra schools and enforce attendance as far as was possible. To pay for all this parish education there was a charge of around 3d (1p) a week, but after the Education Act of 1890 elementary education was virtually 'free' in that it came out of a local rate levied for education. Up to the 1872 Act the schools in St Andrews were a mixture of private schools of various kinds of which 'adventure' schools were the most curious. From long before the Reformation men and women had established 'adventure' schools, so called because they were a financial 'adventure'; the schools were run by many who had only a smattering of education themselves. It was not unusual for tradesmen, from cobblers to public-house keepers, to run a school from these establishments. For young ladies and gentlemen of the middle class and the gentry there were private schools run by many an untrained 'Dame' or 'Gentleman of Letters'. A glance at a national directory of 1873 shows the list of schools in St Andrews to include that of the Misses Moir for young ladies at 4 Alexandra Park, Thomas Hodges at West View, Annie Morton, 42 North Street and the Rev Jack George of Seaton House. Miss Murray ran a school on the site of the Tudor Café and several of the children of the poor received instruction at the hospital at South Lodge.

Several of the private schools were of the highest probity. Such included Dr Fogo's Boys' School, Edgecliff, The Scores, run 1889−1906; and Kilrule Private School for Girls at 140 Market Street which was in existence until 1900; Dr Cleghorn's Academy was sited at 5 Alexandra Place and Dr John Browning's boarding school was at St Leonards House. All the town's private schools prepared boys for the university, the armed services and the Indian civil service as well as boarding boys and girls whose families worked abroad.

The first small private school of any note was started in St Andrews by Dr J. Smeaton (d.1871), who had come to the burgh in the 1840s and was a teacher at Madras. He commenced his school in Market Street and purchased Abbey

Alfred George Le Maitre (1866–1943), and his wife and elder daughter, pose with the Class of 1930 at St Salvator's School, at 2 The Scores (on the site of the present Scores Hotel). Le Maitre had purchased the school, founded in 1881, in 1903 and developed it into a prominent preparatory school for boarders and day boys (*Miss Laura Le Maitre*).

Park around 1869. In 1889 the Abbey Park Institution for Young Gentlemen was transferred to Leask, and the site was taken over by St Leonard's School.

Clifton Bank school was founded around 1860 by John Paterson, another master from Madras, and this was taken over by Messrs Macmillan and Lawson in 1892, and then by Walter G. Mair, also a former teacher at Madras in 1904. Clifton Bank, set on The Scores, survived until 1917 when its building was taken over by St Katherine's junior school. Perhaps the school's most famous former pupil was Field Marshal the Earl Haig of Bemersyde, the commander-in-chief of World War I.

St Salvator's School at 2 The Scores (on the site of the present Scores Hotel) was founded in 1881 by one Gerald Blunt, who remained its headmaster until 1903. Two supporters of Blunt's enterprise were Professor William Knight, Professor of Moral Philosophy and Political Economy, and Emeritus Professor Lewis Campbell, Professor of Greek, through whose influence the school's name was allowed by the university. In 1903 the school was purchased by Alfred George Le Maitre (1866–1943), who developed it into a prominent preparatory school for boarders and day boys. The school was classics orientated with no science being taught at all, and the maximum number of boys at any one time was 50, who were prepared for such public schools as Fettes and Sedbergh and for the Royal Navy (entry in those days was at 12½ years old). The school did not have its own playing fields but rented ground (then known as Mount Pleasant) from the Strathtyrum estates, which was located where the Madras playing fields are today. The school hospice was at 9 Golf Place (once Kirk's Place). Alfred Le Maitre sold the school in 1931 to Mrs King who developed it into a hotel. The school trophies and cups were purchased by Lathallan School who absorbed the pupils then being educated at the time of the sale.

Of the town's schools one of the most interesting was the Fisher School, known also as the 'East Infants' (1856). The fishing community of mariners, fish-curers, pilots, fishermen and so on supported a school for their own children, although pupils from 4–14 years of age who attended were not solely from fisher stock (in fact in the 1850s there were complaints that burgh children were holding places in the school which should have gone to fisher children). The school opened in the evenings for sewing and the '3Rs' as many of the children worked during the day baiting the lines.

St Andrews has long been in the forefront of the development of education of women. Here in 1862 Elizabeth Garrett Anderson (1836–1917) obtained the support which

The courtyard of St Leonard's School (founded 1877) which moved to this site in 1882. The whole site had been that of St Leonard's College (1512), which was sold by the University in the 18th century. To the right is the site of the original college hall of *circa* 1590; facing is the building of 1901; and to the left the Dr William Guild Building of 1655.

was to lead her to become the first English woman to enter the medical profession, and in the 1860s there evolved the idea to found a public school for girls in the burgh. Who had the idea first is hard to say, but certainly it was mooted in the social circle in which the widow and daughters of Dr Cook, Professor of Hebrew, were wont to circulate. In 1868 Miss Harriet Cook was present at an occasion in Miss Elizabeth Garrett's house in London when the possibility of forming a women's college at Cambridge was discussed; this was eventually to develop into Girton College (1869), and two of its students, Rachel Cook and Louisa Innes Lumsden, were to be involved in the school for girls that was to be founded in St Andrews. The fact that these women passed the Classical

Tripos at Cambridge — the first women to do so — caused a stir in St Andrews, and this and the fact that Miss Cowan's school for girls in Queen Street (today's Queens Gardens) was to close, gave the promotion of a new school for girls in St Andrews a great boost.

Practical plans for a girls' school at St Andrews were formulated at Kirnan, the home of Lewis Campbell, Professor of Greek. Leading lights were Mrs Lewis Campbell and Mrs Matthew Rodger, the wife of the minister of St Leonards parish, and the members of the Ladies Education Association. Approaches were made to Miss Lumsden and her friend Miss Constance Maynard — also of Girton — to assist in the setting up of the school and on 15 January 1877 a Council was formed for the St Andrews School for Girls Company. So on 2 October 1877, in the building which now houses St Regulus university residence in Queens Gardens, the school was established with Miss Louisa Lumsden as the first headmistress. The school was funded by shares taken up by individuals and income from school fees, and a total of 50 girls enrolled in 1877 of whom ten were boarders. The school offered a high standard of academic subjects and provided a gymnasium and playground which was unheard of in Victorian Scotland, and it was regarded askance by the residents of Queen Street. It is interesting to note that gymnastic lessons (known in Scotland as 'physical drill') did not appear in the Scottish Day School Code until 1895. In 1927 Dame Louisa Lumsden, as she had now become, herself summed up the spirit of the emergent school: 'Truth was its inspiration, truth in thought and deed and word. Intellectual work was to be thorough, not slight or shallow, but honest, which of course means hard. Play was to have its fitting place, it too was not to be frivolous but in its way as honest as work. The girls were to learn to govern themselves, to be worthy of trust and to be trusted, and the older and leading girls were to be responsible for a share in government.'

Louisa Lumsden resigned as headmistress in 1878 but remains the most prominent 'personality' in the school's

Girls from St Leonard's School walk past St Leonard's Chapel, once a part of St Leonard's College (1512). The chapel was re-roofed in 1910 and a complete renovation was inaugurated in 1948, to be re-dedicated in 1952. To the right is the gateway leading to the Nun's Walk, named after a ghost.

history. She was to continue to be a prominent figure in St Andrews too; from 1895 to 1900 she was warden of University Hall and in 1925 she was created DBE; one commentator writing in the press about her state honour described her as 'of the race of those great adventurers and pioneers who have made the British Empire what it is'. Dame Louisa died in 1935, aged 95, but remains in prominence as a 'character' in the annual Kate Kennedy procession.

The school remained in Queen Street until 1882 when it moved into the house and grounds of the old Playfair residence of St Leonards, Pends Road, from which it drew its new name. Today the school properties cover some 30 acres of parkland roughly bounded by Pends Road and Kinnessburn, although some of its southern acres were sold in the late 1980s for development as Greenside Court. The school's main buildings, apart from the swimming pool, science and main school blocks include the former residence of Principal James Forbes, Bishophall (1862; College Hall 1868, then Bishophall the residence of Charles Wordsworth, 1806−92, Bishop of St Andrews, Dunkeld and Dunblane, until the school bought it in 1887; extended 1936); St Rules (1895−96) − both of these buildings front the remains of the Priory guest house of *circa* 1350; the Hospice (1894), on the site of the *Hospitium Novum*; St Katherine's (Sanatorium, 1899 on the Abbey Mill site; extended 1974); St Nicholas (1930); Abbey Park House (1815; extended 1853; taken over by the school in 1889); St Leonard's (in the) Fields (1927) and Queen Mary's House.

In 1894 a preparatory school was opened in the Georgian house at 91 North Street under the name of St Katherine's to replace the junior department at Priorsgate. The house had been built *circa* 1815 with extensions of 1830 and retains its portico with four columns. When St Katherine's was sold the building was developed in 1978 as a Centre for the Arts. St Leonard's School badge and motto remember the old Priory associations in that they incorporate the motto *Ad Vitam*, the crosier and shield of Prior James Hepburn.

A private school for boys was established at New Park, Hepburn Gardens in 1933 by Cuthbert Dixon (d.1949), formerly of the Merchiston Preparatory School. It was to remain an all male staff school until World War II when a 'petticoat brigade' of women joined; among these teachers was Willa Muir, the wife of the poet Edwin Muir (1887−1959). The school was extended in 1936, and originally incorporated the old Plash Mill Cottage (now known as New Park Cottage), parts of which date from 1658, utilised by the janitor. Today the school admits female pupils.

Apart from Madras, St Leonard's and New Park, the burgh is served today by Canongate Primary School (1971), Maynard Road, Langlands School (1957), Kilrymont Road and Lawhead Primary (1974), Strathkinness Low Road. The teaching of Roman Catholic children in terms of their own religious instruction was done largely outside school hours in various school buildings in the town. A Catholic Primary School, however, was opened in 1959 staffed by Poor Clares of Newry, under the title of Greyfriars School, with teaching rooms at the church hall of St James's Church on the Scores; teaching was subsequently moved to a house in Queens Terrace. In 1968 the school was taken over by Fife Education Authority and was moved into the old Board School (1889) in Abbey Street in 1969; this time it was staffed by lay teachers.

CHAPTER 10

Victorian and Edwardian St Andrews
and its Characters

Queen Victoria was the last member of the House of Hanover and she was born at Kensington Palace on 24 May 1819, the only child of HRH Prince Edward, Duke of Kent and Strathearn (1767–1820), and his wife, Her Serene Highness Mary Louisa Victoria of Saxe-Coburg-Saalfeld (1786–1861). Victoria ascended the throne on 20 June 1837 on the death of her uncle William Henry, Duke of Clarence (b.1765), who had joined the Royal Navy as a midshipman of thirteen and had ruled as William IV from 1830 – 'Sailor Billy' he was to some and 'Silly Billy' to others in recognition of his naivety and Hanoverian lack of intellect. William IV was the last monarch to have the name of St Andrews in a title. His father, George III, had created him Duke of Clarence and St Andrews in 1789 and the title had merged with the crown in 1830. The use of the town in a royal title remained dormant until in October 1934 King George V created his fourth son, HRH Prince George, Duke of Kent, the Earl of St Andrews on the occasion of his marriage to Princess Marina of Greece. The prince was a frequent visitor to St Andrews in the mid-1930s to be honoured by the university in 1936 and to play-in as Captain of the Royal and Ancient Golf Club in 1937. Prince George's grandson, George Philip Nicholas, born in 1962, holds the title today.

Victoria was crowned at Westminster Abbey on 28 June 1838 and in St Andrews there were great rejoicings with representative processions made up of municipal dignitaries, freemasons and schoolchildren. Arches of flowers hung across Union Street and bunting festooned St Rule's Tower and the Castle, adding to the colour of the day, and bonfires lit up the evening sky; throughout the day junketing took place in both public house and middle-class parlour alike and food was distributed to the poor. On 10 February 1840 Victoria married her cousin HRH Prince Albert of Saxe-Coburg and Gotha (1819−61) and by then the town had settled down to a new era.

During the autumn of 1876 St Andrews folk were all-a-gog as it was fixed that on Wednesday 27 September, HRH Prince Leopold would visit the burgh to be installed as Captain of the Royal and Ancient. Leopold, Duke of Albany (1853−84), the haemophiliac eighth child and fourth son of Queen Victoria, married Princess Helena of Waldeck-Pyrmont (1861−1922) in 1882, and they became the parents of the very popular HRH Princess Alice, Countess of Athlone (1883−1981). Prince Leopold was looked upon as a 'Scottish adoptee' as his title had originated in 1398, in the reign of Robert III; Mary Queen of Scots had bestowed it on Henry Darnley and it had descended through the Hanoverian line to Leopold. The prince duly arrived and was hosted by John Whyte-Melville of Mount Melville and he was installed as Royal and Ancient captain, and Provost Walter Thomas Milton was presented. The prince lunched with Principal Tulloch and visited St Mary's College with a walk to the cathedral, the castle and an unexpected call at the Ladyhead to meet the fisherfolk. He dined at the Royal and Ancient and the next day he attended a meet of the Fife Fox Hounds at Mount Melville, played golf and appeared at a civic ball at the Town Hall. Leopold was presented with an album of photographs by Thomas Rodger Jr and was much taken by the bonfires, street decorations and warmth of welcome. Accompanied by his equerry, The Hon. Alexander Grantham Yorke, who wrote letters of thanks to the provosts of St Andrews and Cupar, Leopold left St Andrews station on 29th September, walking through a guard of honour mounted by the St Andrews Artillery Company. This had been the first royal visit since that of Charles II. Leopold returned in 1877 and photographic studio portraits of him were taken by Thomas Rodger which are still to be found in the Royal Archives at Windsor.

St Andrews, incidentally, was in the forefront of the birth of photography in Scotland, because of the mutual interests of three men, Sir David Brewster (1781—1868), Principal of the United College, William Henry Fox Talbot (1800—77), the English inventor and practitioner of the calotype photographic process, and Dr John Adamson (1809—70), soon to be Medical Officer of Health of St Andrews. They joined to promote photography in Scotland and Dr Adamson produced the first calotype taken in Scotland in May 1840. The first commercial studio in Fife was that set up in 1849 by Thomas Rodger in the vicinity of Abbey Street.

Prince Leopold's visit and other events were recorded in great detail by the *St Andrews Citizen*, a newspaper which had its birth in 1870. The *Fife Herald* (1823) had developed from Robert Tullis's *Cupar Herald* in 1822 and in 1870 the managing editor of the *Fife Herald* and *Fife News,* John Innes, instituted a St Andrews edition of the *Fife News* which was to be amalgamated with the *Fife Herald* in 1910. The *Fife Herald* had absorbed its main rival in the area, the *Fifeshire Journal,* in 1893. In 1879 John Innes purchased the whole business and the properties of the printer Robert Tullis (1775—1831) of St Andrews. Thus 'St Andrews-orientated news' was promulgated from a small house and printing shop at the corner of South Street and Church Street; this included the post office run by Provost George Murray (d.1908) which was moved to new premises next door in 1892. The post office site, incidentally, was the home of the Christian Institute from 1907 to 1953. The print shop was rebuilt at the Citizen Office in 1928 and the shop next door was absorbed in 1965. Here too had been the type foundry (1742—44) and birthplace of Adam Bell in 1753. The town was also catered for in news reportage by the *St Andrews Gazette* which ran from 1862—63, then as the *St Andrews Gazette & Fifeshire News* until 1883.

The St Andrews Pictorial Magazine was first published in 1831; its contents were of general and national interest, with short stories, fashion notes, travel, natural history and puzzles; basically there was little local material published apart from births, marriages and deaths. However, the publisher in 1859, P. Thomson of 51 South Street, included a plea for 'anything not generally known in the history of any of the old buildings in the town. . . .'

Travel for the Victorian St Andrean was restricted to private carriage and gig, hired coaches, or a weekly public coach between the town and Cupar; and a twice-weekly coach from such inns as the Black Bull (at 27 South Street — the old Co-op buildings — and until 1840 it was the town's chief hostelry; it closed in 1850). This, of course, supplemented the much used sea transport from St Andrews harbour and the Eden port.

Fife's first passenger railway was opened on 29 June 1847 from Burntisland to Cupar and Lindores by the Edinburgh and Northern Railway Co. This company developed as the Edinburgh, Perth and Dundee Railway in 1849, to be taken over by the North British Railway in 1862 (LNER, 1923; British Railways, 1948) and it was the E,P&DR company which operated the St Andrews railway. When this railway opened St Andrews travellers were picked up by local coaches for the link to and from Leuchars. In 1850 the St Andrews Railway Co was formed to link Leuchars with St Andrews, via Guardbridge, and the line was opened by the directors, said the *Fifeshire Journal,* on 29 May 1852. The town's first station was located on the site of the modern Old Course Hotel and Country Club and was known as Links Station. Under the date 3 July 1852 *The Scotsman* recorded the opening of the St Andrews line: 'This event, highly important not only for the town of St Andrews, but for the whole of Fife, took place on Tuesday at midday. Strangers, especially those belonging to the chief towns in the county, had been invited by the directors to be present. A number of additional first class carriages had been provided to conduct them along the main line to Leuchars. When the Leuchars station was reached, a little after twelve o'clock, the directors, Mr Ellice [*Edward Ellice MP*] and a large number of the inhabitants were there to receive the strangers, and accompany them along the new line to St Andrews. After a short delay, incident on the exchange of courtesies, all took their seats. They filled some eight or ten first class carriages. On starting, the Leuchars folks, crowds of whom had gathered at the station, cheered loudly and lustily. The progress was both swift and smooth. The time occupied in travelling from Leuchars to St Andrews station was between thirteen and fourteen minutes. At the station a number of ladies and gentlemen of St Andrews were waiting. A dinner took place in the Town Hall at which seventy-three gentlemen were present. Mr Ellice MP was in the chair and the talent and affability of the honourable gentlemen carried the company quickly and smoothly along. He was supported on the right by Major Playfair of St Andrews, and Provost Sang of Kirkcaldy, and on the left by the Rev. Dr. Buist and Prof. Alexander. Mr. W. F. Ireland and Mr Alex Meldrum, Easter Kincaple, officiated as croupiers. The line was opened on Thursday for regular traffic. The fares are extremely moderate. The railway has been made cheaply, and is to be travelled very cheaply.' The cost of building the railway had been £5,625 by the notorious Sir Thomas Bouch whose Tay Bridge collapsed in 1879. By 1857 the journey from St Andrews to Leuchars was twenty minutes, and in 1877 the line was absorbed into the North British Railway.

On 16 July 1883 there was an authorisation for a link between Anstruther and St Andrews Railway and the North British Railway at St Andrews, but only by 1 June 1887 was the link completed via Kingsbarns and Boarhills. The link between St Andrews and Boarhills which opened in 1883 was made by coach operated by the Rusack family, then proprietors of the Star Hotel. St Andrews now had a new station situated nearer the town centre than the Links, off City Road. When the Forth Bridge was opened on 4 March

Gibson Hospital, Argyle Street, remains a fine example of Victorian building enterprise in St Andrews. Projected and endowed by Bailie William Gibson of Dunloch, for the 'aged sick, and infirm poor', the hospital was opened in 1884 and remains a home for the retired.

1890, St Andrews had convenient links with Edinburgh and the south. All of which led to the further opening up of the East Neuk to tourists and increasingly speedy deliveries of agricultural and fishery products. The Links Station of 1852—87 became the goods station, with its engine shed, coal yard and offices. The Station Master's house is still retained as the Jigger Inn.

The railway system at St Andrews began to decline in the 1920s when, first, the through services from St Andrews to Perth were closed. The decline was gradual, though; in 1930 the stations of Kingsbarns, Boarhills, Stravithie and Mount Melville were closed to passengers and in 1954 Dairsie station closed. By 1964 the St Andrews to Crail line closed to freight and by 1965 the St Andrews to Leven link was closed to passengers. Freight was also closed in 1966 from Guardbridge to St Andrews and on 6 January 1969 the Leuchars to St Andrews line was finally closed to passengers.

Since 1969 the old railway track has been part developed to the south as car parks and walkways; the short tunnel under Doubledykes Road is sealed, as has been the aperture under the humped-back Lade Braes bridge, and the Canongate bridge was demolished. Today householders in Drumcarrow Road and Spottiswoode Gardens have long purchased the railway embankment for garden extensions. The station site is now a car park and the embankment to the west still abuts Windmill Road, and Petheram Bridge over the line of the modern A91 was demolished; next to the modern footbridge here, by the by, the Victorians had their curling pond where the biblically named Jacob's Ladder path meets the A91 and they played on natural ice but were disturbed by railway workings; a new artificial pond was constructed at Law Mill in 1905. St Andrews Curling Club formed in 1846.

A prominent transportation group in Victorian St Andrews was the Carters, also known as the Whiplickers, whose society had been re-established in 1872. St Andrews' carters had been extant as a group from the Middle Ages, when they struck their bargains before the altar to their patron St Michael, set in Holy Trinity church. The rendezvous of the carters, on the day they held their annual races, was the 'Blue Stane', which used to be in the middle of the road across from Hope Park church; today the old whinstone nestles by the railings in the garden of what was the Alexandra, then Station Hotel, at the northwest of Alexandra Place. The Blue Stane's origins are unknown, but tradition dates it from Pictish St Andrews where it may have been a boundary stone for the ecclesiastical enclave. One local myth tells how a giant, angry at the influence of St Rule, picked up the stone at Blebo Craigs and threw it at the saint's cell on the Kirkhill. The stone fell short and landed at the end of Market Street. The stone has had various locations from Magus Muir to the West Port and tradition invested it with sanctity down the years of such potency that hoary farmers doffed their hats to it, the pikemen off to Bannockburn in 1314 patted it for luck, and women curtseyed to it — or so the old folk said. For a number of years, after its foundation in 1880, a Coachman's Ball was held in St Andrews for the coachmen in the area.

Politically, Victorian St Andrews was served by only four MPs. Parliamentary representation of St Andrews is associated with the rise of the burgesses into the Third Estate in the early part of the fourteenth century; before that St Andrews was represented by its bishops, priors and provosts. From the Great Council, held at Cambuskenneth in 1326, the burgh was known to be represented as an entity and from 1357 there are named MPs known. The earliest recorded MPs to date for which there are records were Adam of Kirkytolach and Lawrence Bell both serving around 1357, with Wilyame Bonar representing the town during 1456—68. In the sixteenth century there were the following MPs: David Learmonth to 1524; James Learmonth 1524—44; Sir Patrick Learmonth 1567—68; Leonard Williams 1572; Thomas

Walwood 1578; David Russell 1579 and 1590; Patrick Learmonth 1581 and 1585; Duncan Balfour 1583; William Russell 1586 and 1598; William Murray 1594; and David Forret 1599. During the seventeenth century there were fourteen known MPs: John Arnot 1612; Thomas Robertson 1617; Henry Arthur 1621; James Watson 1630; John Lepar 1639−40/1644−46; James Lenton 1646−47; James Robertson 1648; James Sword 1649−51; Andrew Carstairs 1650; Col James Whetham 1656−60; Robert Lenton 1665; John Geddie of St Nicholas 1667−78; John Eassone 1681−86; and James Smith 1689−1702.

From 1707 to the 1832 Reform Act, St Andrews was combined with Forfar, Cupar, Perth and Dundee to share one MP. After the Act, St Andrews Burghs came into being to include Cupar, Crail, Anstruther Easter, Anstruther Wester, Kilrenny and Pittenweem. The first MP under this new scheme was Andrew Johnston of Rennyhill (1798−1862) who was elected for St Andrews in the parliament of 1831 and sat until he retired in 1837. He was followed by Edward Ellice (1810−80), a Liberal in favour of Irish disestablishment who sat until he retired. In 1880 Stephen Williamson of Copely (1827−1903), a Home Rule Liberal, took the seat but he was ultimately defeated in a 'tie' and Henry Torrens Anstruther the Liberal Unionist was declared MP. In Scotland two new university seats were created by the 1867 Reform Act and St Andrews was grouped with Edinburgh. The first MP elected by the Chancellors, the members of the University Courts, professors and members of the General Councils was (Sir) Hugh Lyon Playfair, who served 1868−85 as a Liberal. The first Conservative to win was the Rt. Hon. J. H. A. MacDonald who served from 1885−88; thereafter the Conservatives (as Unionists, Liberal Unionists and Conservative Unionists) predominated. Later the two university seats were combined to represent four universities (St Andrews, Aberdeen, Glasgow and Edinburgh) with three MPs and described as the Scottish Universities constituencies, balloted for by Proportional Representation. The university

An early advertisement for Rusack's Marine Hotel which was founded in 1884 by Johann Wilhelm Christof Rusack (1848–1916) and opened in 1887. The hotel was to become famous in Scotland, patronised by royalty, particularly HRH Edward Prince of Wales and the famous Rothschild financiers as well as such golfing celebrities as Bobby Jones, Bobby Locke and Peter Thomson. The hotel was acquired by the St Andrews Links Trust in 1980 and was sold to Trusthouse Forte in 1985 (*Trusthouse Forte plc*).

seats were abolished by the Representation of the People Act 1948 and no longer appeared after the February 1950 election. Sir James Matthew Barrie was asked to stand for the Liberals for the university seat in 1900, but declined, yet perhaps the most celebrated MP who sat for St Andrews was the writer John Buchan, who served as a Conservative from 1927 to 1935 in which year his appointment as Governor-General of Canada made him ineligible to sit.

Until 1901 St Andrews was served by a town council of twenty three councillors, a provost, three bailies, a Dean of Guild and a treasurer, and most of them were elected by the old town guilds. After 1901 the council was reduced to twelve, to include the provost, two magistrates and a Dean of Guild. The longest serving provost was W. T. Milton (1869—81) and many prominent businessmen and academics served in the office in Victorian and Edwardian times, including John McGregor the furnisher, Professor John Herkless and Andrew Aikman of grocers Aikman and Terras. The provost who served the shortest period was Major C. H. M. Cheape during 1915, and the town had to wait until 1952 to elect its first woman provost in Jessie L. Moir. The town's first woman councillor, elected in 1919, was Frances Jane Warrack (1865—1950). Although David I had given the city and royal burgh of St Andrews the right to use certain ensigns, it was not until 1912 that the town petitioned the Lord Lyon King of Arms to matriculate the city ensigns. The town's provost's chain of office was presented to St Andrews by the Marquis of Bute in 1897.

In terms of public entertainment the Victorians had open-air dancing and swimming at the Step Rock—young men and boys usually swam naked in the sea and a future Archbishop of Canterbury, Cosmo Gordon Lang (he became Archbishop in 1928), remembered bathing naked in the sea at St Andrews during a holiday in the 1870s — and there was a skating rink in operation on the Scores (opposite the Craigmount Nursing Home) from 1875 to 1890. 'Ice-day' holidays in which large numbers of young and old went to Kilconquhar, Strathtyrum and Leuchars to skate were popular too. Musically there was the Choral Society started by Mr Salter, the organist of the Episcopal Church in North Street, in the 1860s, and the City Band was founded in 1879. There were various clubs and associations established too like the St Andrews Burns Club which was instituted on 25 January 1869 at the Royal Hotel on the one hundred and tenth anniversary of the death of the poet. When the new town hall was completed in 1861 the hall above the council chamber was fitted out as a lodge for the local Freemasons; their rooms were completed in 1897. There was a lodge of Freemasons in St Andrews as early as

1600 but the current Lodge 25 dates from the 1720s and is one of the Province of Fife and Kinross.

Victorian St Andrews was to see a new era of building development; the existing roads were widened, new highways were constructed, and buildings were reconstructed or demolished and new ones put in their place. North and South Bell Street evolved between 1834 and 1858, as did Queens Gardens, Gillespie Terrace, Gibson Place and Playfair Terrace. Waggons carrying sandstone from such quarries as those at Blebo Craigs and Strathkinness regularly trundled into the town and permanent employment was offered to St Andrews craftsmen from carpenters to masons during this period. Of the main public buildings erected, the Gibson Hospital is a worthy example of Victorian enterprise in the town, projected and endowed by Bailie William Gibson of Dunloch, as a home for those 'aged sick, and infirm poor' who were natives of St Andrews or St Leonards parishes (these conditions of admission were altered in 1934 to include those who had lived in St Andrews for ten years). Gibson had proposed such an enterprise in the 1860s but it did not come into operation until 23 June 1884. There had been local doubts as to the wisdom of opening such a centre — the Adamson Hospital at Ceres, a similar venture, had just closed because of lack of funds, but these objections were overcome and the foundation stone was laid in 1882 by J. Whyte-Melville, with full masonic honours.

The town also had a burgeoning number of hotels stimulated by the expansion of Victorian tourism of which Rusack's Marine has an interesting family story. By the time that Johann Wilhelm Christof Rusack died in 1916 he had made 'The Marine' hotel into an internationally respected golfing hotel. During his forty-year stay in St Andrews, Rusack saw the ancient burgh develop from a little-known holiday resort into a place of great tourist potential. Born in 1848, Rusack came from the fashionable summer resort of Bad Harzburg, Lower Saxony, and was of Huguenot extraction. His forebears had been of the old French family of De Rousac, Huguenots who had emigrated to Germany from Normandy in the seventeenth century. He came to Britain in 1871 after serving in the Franco-Prussian war, and became a naturalised citizen in 1885. Soon after he arrived in St Andrews, he started up the 'Rusacks Private Hotel', Abbotsford Crescent, and by 1877 he had taken over the former Star Hotel, Market Street. He also ran Kinloch House and the Temperance Hotel. Convinced that St Andrews was to become an important watering place, Rusack acquired a piece of land on the Links in 1884 — ten years exactly after he first came to St Andrews — and on that land was built the Marine Hotel which was opened in 1887. Enlargements were made in 1892 and by 1896 the family were also owners of Bogward Farm which became Rusacks Home Farm. The hotel was to become one of the most famous in Scotland, patronised by royalty, particularly HRH Edward, Prince of Wales, the famous Rothschild financiers and by such golfing celebrities as Bobby Jones, Bobby Locke, Peter Thomson and Kel Nagle, the latter two of whom stayed with their families during the 1984 Open. Even 'James Bond' otherwise known as Sean Connery stayed most years during the autumn. Wilhelm Rusack served on the St Andrews Town Council and was Dean of Guild; he took an active part in the masonic movement. On his death the hotel was carried on by the Rusack family but was ultimately acquired by the St Andrews Links Trust in 1980 and was bought from them in 1985 by Trusthouse Forte Hotels.

St Andrews was to become one of the most 'modern' towns in Britain; the telegraph came to the town in 1870 and the first telephone was obtained by R. Niven, flesher, in 1885. Street lighting in St Andrews was boasted of as 'the best in Scotland', with its distinctive Victorian livery of white and Venetian red. Oil lamps were replaced by gas. Manufacture of gas began in St Andrews in 1835 under the active enterprise of Provost Kirby Dalrymple and a new gas tank was erected in 1878. The St Andrews Gas Co. ceased to exist after October

1949 when it was taken over by the Gas Board, and gas was produced in the town until 23 February 1962 when the works were closed. Electric current was switched on in St Andrews in 1905.

As befitted a town which had won a living from and on the sea, St Andrews was in the forefront of Victorian marine innovation. The first marine laboratory in Britain was established in St Andrews in 1884 at the East Bents and set in the old isolation fever hospital which stood on the site of the present putting green. The research here was directed by Professor William Carmichael McIntosh (1838—1931) and contributed much to marine knowledge internationally. In time the old wooden fever hospital became inconvenient to use and a new laboratory was built in 1896 through the generosity of Dr Charles Henry Gatty (1835—1903). The old hospital, incidentally, survived until it was destroyed by fire in 1905.

Within Westburn Lane — and later to be a private wash-house — was the site of St Andrews' first bank opened in 1792 as a branch of the Bank of Scotland and run by the agents Charles Dempster & Co. This bank was relocated several times but in 1870 it was moved to the corner site of South Street and Queens Gardens. By 1845 St Andrews was served by the Eastern Bank (W. F. Ireland, agent), the Clydesdale (Walter Walker) and the Edinburgh & Leith (Ireland & Murray). A savings bank had been established in St Andrews in the Town Hall in 1846, which was to become the Dundee Savings Bank at 12 Church Street where it had moved in 1921. The 1930 Dundee Savings Bank was reconstructed in 1937 and was taken over in modern times by the Trustee Savings Bank. In 1930 too, the National & Union Bank, South Street (the site of John Menzies's current shop) was opened under the agency of A. Gilchrist of Queens Gardens; the bank's coat of arms remains on the frontage. Today the town is served by two branches of the Bank of Scotland, in South Street and Market Street (in 1971, on the site of the

British Linen Bank of 1903), two branches of the Royal Bank, in South Street and again in Market Street (1857), and the Clydesdale.

Queen Victoria died at Osborne House, Isle of Wight, in the arms of her grandson Kaiser Wilhelm II of Germany, at 6.30 p.m., 22 January 1901. The new king, born Albert Edward, Prince of Wales, on 9 November 1841, was sixty-one years old when he was proclaimed at the Cross of St Andrews, Market Street, on Saturday, 27 January 1901, by Provost James Ritchie Welch who died in 1903. A royal salute was fired by the Voluntary Artillery at Kirkhill, and by this year the folk of St Andrews had gone a long way towards becoming 'Anglicised' in their private and public life. Most of the town's upper strata were educated at English public schools and the town commerce was run along the lines of Anglo-Saxon capitalism interlarded with Calvinist thrift.

All in all St Andrews Edwardian society reflected the affluence and ostentation of the period, and the age of strict social discipline, peace and plenty for those who could afford it. Edward's reign was a time of transition between the leisurely self-confidence of the Victorian Age and the bursting forth of the revolutionary years which were to be heralded by the advent of World War I. But no-one who took part in the coronation festivities in St Andrews on Saturday, 9 August 1902, had an inkling of the coming horrors of Flanders fields. Instead they craned their necks at the official proclamation procession as it wended its way round the town to Divine Service at Holy Trinity and oohed and aahed at the fireworks which burst across the burgh, and strolled under the chinese lanterns and padella lights in South Street and Market Street. St Andrews' administrators had had plenty of time to make their arrangements for the displays, as the coronation had been postponed from 26 June 1902, because the king had had to have an emergency operation for an appendicitis.

The Edwardian Age, then, had begun in the wake of tremendous change; Britain had lost her supremacy in

John-Patrick, 3rd Marquess of Bute (1847–1900), was first elected Rector of St Andrews University in 1892. He became a driving force for expansion in the University and gave large sums of money, for instance, for medical buildings. A devout and prominent Roman Catholic, he spent much time researching, and much cash funding, excavations on the site of the medieval priory. In 1946 his family, the Crichton-Stuarts of Falkland, gave the priory to the state.

foreign commerce and on 13 July 1902 the Victorian Conservative Prime Minister, Lord Salisbury, resigned in favour of A. J. Balfour and in 1905 after a decade out of office, the Liberals were given a mandate to try to satisfy the needs of the people. In 1902 also, there had been a signing of a treaty of alliance between Britain and Japan which underlined the end of that 'splendid isolation' which had been Victorian Britain's international rôle since the Crimean War. But rich and poor St Andreans, Tory or Liberal, all looked to King Edward's reign with great optimism; indeed many believed that it had been Britain's misfortune that Edward had not come to the throne at least ten years earlier.

During the nine years of Edward's reign, St Andrews District constituency was firmly Liberal. At the new parliament of 1901, Henry Torrens Anstruther (1860−1926) was re-elected (he had served since 1886) as a Liberal Unionist and continued until 1903 when he was appointed Director of the Suez Canal. His place was taken by Captain Edward Charles Ellice (1858−1934), Liberal, who was subsequently defeated in 1906 by Major William Anstruther-Gray of Kilmany, the Unionist candidate. In the election of 1910 Anstruther-Gray was defeated by (Sir) James Duncan Millar (1871−1932), Liberal, who sat from January to December 1910, when he was defeated by Anstruther-Gray, who represented the constituency until he retired in 1918.

Edwardian St Andrews was a place of bustle and the burgh streets reflected the clutter of the average home. People were out and about from the early hours, the first on the pavements being the milk vendors, the bakers with their baskets of steaming baps, and the home produce sellers. It was a scene of noise with the wheels and horses of drays, carriages and carts being the noisiest. By eight o'clock in the morning the itinerants were out; the knife grinders, the pan menders and the fish sellers all jostling for business. Folks were busy, but wages were low and the distress was only too apparent if you went down such places as Crail's Lane and Abbey Street; the extent of the state of the poor was to be brought into focus by Conservative Prime Minister A. J. Balfour's Royal Commission on the Poor Law and the Relief of Distress by 1905. Half of the burgh's town houses had one or two rooms with shared extra-mural sanitation. Many were dark, draughty, cramped, malodorous and vermin infested. A two-roomed house in South Castle Street could cost as much as 3/6 (17½p) per week, while a one-roomed cottage would fetch 1/- (5p). This was a high sum for an unskilled worker on 18/- (90p) a week. Wages were by no means equitable for physical work done; a full-time shop assistant at W. M. Greig, outfitters of 65 South Street, might earn £30 per year, while a science master at Madras could command £140. But most people settled in St Andrews to the average 22/− (£1.10) a week pay of the farm worker. The standard of living of such families as that of the Very Rev. Principal Alexander Stewart of St Mary's was dependant on a low rate of income tax (1/- in the £ above £160 per annum) and on the plentiful supply of domestic servants. A maid in St Andrews might earn £12 a year, with ambitions to climb the dizzy heights of being a local lawyer's housekeeper at £80 a year.

The Boer War − begun in 1899, the worst war Britain had ever suffered with over 100,000 casualties, and conducted by an army that was half-starved at times − ended on 31 May 1902 and the nation wanted to forget. The *St Andrews Citizen* had published updates of the war's progress and the *Fife News Almanac* had printed regular galleries of the prominent local war dead. A memorial fountain of polished Peterhead granite, made in Aberdeen, was set up at the junction of Logies Lane and South Street (the memorial is now sited in Kinburn Park, by the bowling green) and reads:

DEDICATED TO MAJOR GENERAL R. S. BADEN-POWELL AND THE OTHER IMMORTAL HEROES AND HEROINES OF MAFEKING.
We shall tell our sons your story,
How facing a hostile world:
Starving, fighting, and dying
You kept your flag unfurled:
And the length and breadth of the Empire,
Today with thanksgivings ring,

In praise to the God of Battles
            CHRISTIAN BURKE
For the Heroes of Mafeking.
18th May 1900.

One local Boer War casualty was the golfer Freddy Tait (Lt. F. G. Tait), born in 1870, who was killed at Koodoosberg on 7 February 1900. His name was to be linked with one of Edwardian St Andrews' prominent building projects.

The first hospital in St Andrews, since the Middle Ages, was sited in a rented house in Abbey Street, a memorial to Lady William Keith Douglas of Dunino and Grangemuir, Pittenweem, who died in 1864. Thereafter the town hospital was always referred to as the 'Memorial'. Then, South Lodge, in Abbotsford Place, was acquired using money suscribed for memorials to Dr John Adamson and Dr Oswald Home Bell. The hospital had female wards paid for out of a memorial fund set up by the Douglas family and the male wards were financed out of the Adamson-Bell fund. South Lodge was used as a hospital from 1871, but by the turn of the century it proved too inadequate in size and facilities and a proposal was launched for a new hospital in Abbey Street, on ground feued from George Bruce. The Cottage Hospital was opened on Wednesday, 27 August 1902, by the mother of F. G. Tait whose memorial fund was a principal financial plank, and the Freddy Tait memorial ward was named within the hospital in recognition. The original hospital, on the site of a cottage then by the old sea beach which stretched way up the Kinness Burn, was in the form of a T and cost £3000. Because of the stipulations of donations certain groups of patients were given preferential treatment, namely professional golfers, caddies and (Black Watch) soldiers. Extensions were made to the hospital in 1924, 1927, 1931 and 1938 and the hospital was upgraded during 1987 – 88.

Donations to the hospital flooded in and one benefactor was Major Donald Lindsay Carnegie (1840 – 1911), who lived in a house he built in 1873 in Playfair Terrace; he furnished the hospital surgery and supplied the X-ray apparatus. Major Carnegie also presented an ambulance waggon to the burgh in 1906, commissioned from Reid the coachbuilders of Perth, and he also gifted a Merryweather fire engine to the town in 1901, and one of its first jobs was to put out a fire at the old Links Station. The town, of course, had secured its first fire engine at the Crawford Priory sale of 1834 and bought a replacement in 1865; a Leyland fire engine was bought in 1921 (the 1865 and 1901 fire engines are still retained in store).

Hospital health care in St Andrews was supplemented with the opening of the Infectious Diseases Hospital at St Michaels (now the Pinewoods Hotel), Leuchars, in August 1909, and the town was to be in the forefront of pioneer medical research. In 1919 Sir James Mackenzie (1853–1925) founded the James Mackenzie Institute in the Scores (in the house known as Seaton House, the actual building today being the annexe of the Scores Hotel), an establishment way ahead of its time. Sir James was a prominent heart specialist and pioneered investigative clinical procedures towards a basis of preventive medicine. With the help of local GPs, Sir James held regular meetings at the Scores clinic and established a thorough set of medical records of St Andrews people. This work was carried on into the 1940s when the research endowment passed to the university faculty of Medicine (and allied academic disciplines) and the Child Care Centre at Dyersbrae. One of Mackenzie's assistants at the Institute was to become one of St Andrews' most celebrated doctors. James Orr (1876–1937) first came to St Andrews in 1900 to be a partner in the general practice of Dr Norman McLeod. He is professionally remembered as a fine clinician of the Institute and bought New Park (which became New Park School in 1933) from his distinguished colleague.

It was an era of cleanliness and fresh air activities too, and the new Ladies' Bathing Pond was opened opposite the Castle Bathing Station in 1904. This site had been used as a ladies' bathing pond from around 1845; here too on the cliff was the site of the public baths of around 1811, bought by St Leonard's School for their private use in 1920, the year they bought Castlecliff (*circa* 1877 and now university departments of English and Spanish).

The main areas of building in Edwardian St Andrews were in Bridge Street, Murray Park, Links Crescent with City Road and Pilmour Links, Hepburn Gardens with Kennedy Gardens and Donaldson Gardens, to satisfy a population nudging seven thousand by 1914. At the beginning of the Edwardian era St Andrews was to see a new Caddy Master's Shelter in 1904 at the Links, a pavilion of the St Andrews Bowling Club in 1903, the Parish Church Hall in 1902, Greenside Place, the University Pavilion in 1908, Hepburn Gardens, and the Carnegie Library in 1906 in St Mary's Quad.

For entertainment there were concerts, readings and lectures for the St Andrews Edwardians along with visits from concert parties, famous singers' recitals, Sir Robert Fossett's circus, and cinematograph shows at the Town Hall; the first permanent cinema was the 'Cinema House' of 1913 in North Street, which was followed in 1930 by the 'New Picture House' further along the street. Public lectures were very popular too and large audiences were the norm, particularly for such speakers as Sir Ernest Shackleton (1874–1922), the British explorer who made four Antarctic expeditions and who lectured at St Andrews in 1910.

It was a society of voracious readers and intellectual stimulation for the townsfolk was on every hand. Two citizens were prominent among the town as opposed to gown *literati*, both men of divergent character and capability, in Dr David Hay Fleming and W. T. Linskill. David Hay Fleming had been born on 9 May 1849 the son of a South Street china merchant. Educated at Madras College, he followed a business career, but wealth inherited in 1883 allowed him to devote himself to academic study, local and Reformation history in particular. Elected to the Town Council in 1881, Hay Fleming moved from 177 South Street in 1889 to 16 North

The Martyrs Monument, the Scores, erected in 1842 to the design of the Edinburgh architect William Nixon (c.1810–48). It commemorates the Protestants Paul Craw (1433), Patrick Hamilton (1528), Henry Forrest (1533), George Wishart (1546), and Walter Myln (1558), who were martyred for their faith in St Andrews.

Bell Street (now Greyfriars Garden) and was made a Doctor of Laws of St Andrews university in 1898. He spent the latter years of his life at 4 Chamberlain Road, Edinburgh, where he had moved in 1905. David Hay Fleming was Secretary of the Scottish History Society and made a visit to America in 1907. His *Guidebook* (1881) to St Andrews was the standard guide for some seventy years and his work as Honorary Curator of the cathedral museum — developed from the museum of 1840 jointly sponsored by the Literary and Philosophical Society of St Andrews and the University Court and situated at University College — greatly promoted local history studies and conservation in the burgh.

Up to the work done by Hay Fleming, incidentally, very little had been written about St Andrews in book form for the interested enquirer. Indeed from the seventeenth century to the early nineteenth century only three 'histories' had been written. George Martine of Claremont had produced his *Reliquiae Divi Andreae* in 1683, but this was more of a history of the See of St Andrews than the town, for Martine was probably secretary to Archbishop Sharp. His manuscript lay in sheaves until 1797 when it was prepared for print by Professor John Rotheram of the Natural Philosophy Dept, and was printed by the university printer. In 1807 the Rev. James Grierson produced the first general history of St Andrews under the title *Delineation of St Andrews,* while in 1838 the Rev. J. C. Lyon, presbyter of the Episcopal Church, St Andrews, produced the first standard history. In 1911 there was produced the useful *Handbook to the City and University of St Andrews* by James Maitland Anderson who became chief university librarian. Anderson was born at Rossie, near Collessie in 1852, the son of James Anderson, gardener to Captain James Maitland RN. He started life as a cowherd and became a newspaper reporter and teacher of shorthand, entering the university library in 1873; Anderson died at his residence at Kinnessburn East in 1927, a true Fife 'lad o' pairts'.

Hay Fleming himself died on 7 November 1931 and his

valuable personal library of over 12,000 volumes was bequeathed to the town as the Hay Fleming Reference Library; these were stored by the University Library until the County leased Kinburn House after which they were placed on the top floor of the present public library. The public library of today, incidentally, developed on the eighteenth century site of the English school, which was used as an infant school 1832−44; it then opened as the City Hall in 1845 and was used as a drill hall and auction hall; the City Hall was reconstructed in 1927 for gas offices and so on. The libraries moved in during 1951; next door was the town reservoir of 1819 which subsequently became a fire station and latterly public conveniences. The County Library moved from Queens Gardens to City Hall in 1962.

William T. Linskill was a different character altogether from David Hay Fleming. The son of Captain W. Linskill, Mayor of Tynemouth, and his wife the daughter of Viscount Valentia, Linskill was born in 1855 and was educated at Jesus College, Cambridge. He was brought to St Andrews for holidays in his teens and made the town his home in 1897. Although he had a good working knowledge of the town's history, Linskill's vivid imagination often got the better of him and he went in search of secret passages and lost treasure in the castle and the cathedral precincts. Elected to the Town Council, he became Dean of Guild and played a prominent part in the civic and social scene of the town; he was the driving force behind the St Andrews 'howkers' (Scottish for 'diggers') who dug indiscriminately in the cathedral and castle ruins. A devout Episcopalian and of uncertain temper, Linskill was tutored in golf by young Tom Morris and never tired of telling listeners how he escaped from the Tay Bridge Disaster. Linskill is best remembered today for his fanciful *St Andrews Ghost Stories* which he retold with relish; he borrowed his stories from established legends elsewhere and from his own colourful imagination. Linskill died on 22 November 1929.

At the other end of the social scale were such 'literary

characters' as 'Donald Blue'. Born in 1846, Donald Blue's real name was James McDonald and he was delivered of his mother Margaret Scott at the roadside somewhere between Pittenweem and St Andrews, or so he said; McDonald was brought up by Mrs Watters of Baker Lane. She dressed him in a bright blue jacket, from which he received his life-long nickname. Educated at Madras College as a free scholar, McDonald was somewhat mentally retarded and held multifarious jobs from ship's cook on a Baltic steamer to a labourer on the Burntisland harbour works. He married around 1891 and at the end of his career worked at the Links; an inmate of one of the town's lodging houses, McDonald died in 1909 and was accorded a pauper's funeral. For years people remembered 'Donald Blue's philosophy' — his maxims were common gossip and included these:

'Gouff's guid enuf if yer no a caddie.'

'It's a camsteerie warl' this, ye dinna ken wither it's a saxpence or a broken leg ye're tae get the morn's morning'.

'A wee drappie's a' richt enuf, but ower mony drappies are no easy managed. Hooiver, aye wauk as strecht as ye can'.

Those who wished to participate in leisuretime activities, rather than play a passive rôle, could join the St Andrews Rifle Volunteer Pipe Band, begun in the early 1900s by Pipe-Major Benzie of the 93rd Sutherland Highlanders. The St Andrews Volunteers, by the by, founded in 1859, were disbanded in 1908 and many joined the new Territorial Force (1908), which was to become the Territorial Army in 1920.

Celebrated visitors to St Andrews at this period included General William Booth (1829–1912), founder of the Salvation Army, who held a meeting at the Town Hall in 1908; he was welcomed by the town council and drew a huge street crowd. The suffragettes (members of the Women's Suffrage Movement who agitated to get the parliamentary vote for women) also met in St Andrews Town Hall and at Martyrs Monument and were barracked by the students; the prominent English suffragette, Mrs Emmeline Pankhurst (1858—1928), visited the town in 1910 and 1911, to enjoy addressing a meeting lit by the Town Hall's first electric lights of 1909.

The Edwardian Age ended on 6 May 1910 when Edward VII died at a quarter to midnight at Buckingham Palace. His son was proclaimed as George V at St Andrews on Tuesday, 9 May and the town prepared for the coronation parties. These were held on 22 June 1911 and the civic junketing went on all day, with bonfires at the Bruce Embankment and the harbour, and bunting festooned every street. Coronation mugs, medals and a new penny were given to St Andrews schoolchildren and a loaf, a cake, tea and sundry grocery parcels were given to the poor along with a new shilling; the choice of a jar of Bovril (hailed in *The Illustrated Sporting and Dramatic News* of 1 March 1890 as one of 'Two Infallible Powers: The Pope and Bovril') or a bottle of port was given to the 'invalid poor'. But soon the seemingly ordered, prosperous and sunny days of Edward's reign were to become only a nostalgic memory. Many of the boys who linked with the girls in merry dance down the Scores on Coronation Day were to be slaughtered in the mud on the Franco-Belgian border just three short years away.

CHAPTER 11

A Game for Gentlemen

The Old Course, St Andrews, was deemed 'the worst course on earth' by Bobby Jones when he first competed on it in 1921 — he left half-way through in disgust. Some time later he reflected to the press that the Old Course was 'the very best', and he won the British Open at St Andrews in 1927. The doughty golfer Jack Nicklaus called St Andrews links 'cattle pasture' in 1964, echoing what Sam Snead, the Open Champion in 1946, had said: 'Back home,' remarked Snead, 'we plant beet on land like that'. Yet the truth of the matter is, if a golfer is to be remembered, he or she has to win at St Andrews.

By 1988 golf in St Andrews reached an interesting point in its historical development. For around 1691 the town had been called 'The Metropolis of Golf', but from 1988 a new cliché was being used in describing the town as the 'Golfing Garden of Eden', with plans to make St Andrews the outstanding golf resort in the world. This is all window dressing for the place where, in the whole world of golf, to play has become a religious experience. Indeed the 6545-yard long Old Course has become such sanctified turf, that visitors can be seen stuffing divots into their golf bags as sacrosanct relics to take home. Today the heart and soul of St Andrews is that ground by Pilmour Links, a 400-acre patch of sandy 'linksand' left behind by centuries of tides, where golf reputations are made and marred in front of a media-world audience of millions.

Up to 1988 St Andrews had four 18-hole golf courses. The Old Course (which extends to 6936 yards when the Open Championships are played), which originally had 22 holes, dates from medieval times and up to the eighteenth century ran at least as far as Murray Park. The earliest known survey

The 18th green (Tom Morris Hole) of the Old Course with the Royal & Ancient Clubhouse, which was built in 1854. The R & A does not own any of the St Andrews golf courses, which are run on behalf of the St Andrews Links Trust by the Links Management Committee. In 1989 work began on a new golf museum behind the R & A Clubhouse on the Bruce Embankment.

of the Old Course was made in 1821 but the 1836 survey reduced it to 18 holes; teeing grounds were introduced in 1846, and a green staff was employed by then. There have been few changes to the course since 1913, and there is still no Sunday play.

The New Course (6516 yards) was constructed by the Royal & Ancient Golf Club in 1895. The Jubilee Course was built by the Town Council in 1897 to celebrate Queen Victoria's Diamond Jubilee. This originally consisted of 12 holes, but was increased to 18 in 1912; a reconstruction of the course was undertaken in 1936 by Willie Auchterlonie, Open

185

Champion in 1893 and Hon. Professional of the Royal & Ancient Golf Club, 1935–63. The course was extended and improved in 1981. The Eden Course (6150 yards) was set out by the Town Council in 1912 and the Eden Tournament takes place there each August. The Balgove Course of 9 holes was built in 1971, primarily for use by children and beginners. And, 1988 saw new plans afoot to upgrade the Jubilee Course, alter the Eden Course and build a new 18 hole Strathtyrum Course, all of championship calibre, but remaining public. All this would be enhanced by a futuristic British golf museum funded by the Royal & Ancient Golf Club, all giving St Andrews pre-eminence as the golf shrine of the twenty-first century.

Opinions of the 'playability' of the links at St Andrews have varied down the years. Writing of 1855, David Salmond, one of the proprietors of the *Arbroath Herald*, noted that St Andrews links were very rough. 'There was but one course, and the same nine holes served for the outward as for the inward play. Each hole was marked by a small iron pin, with a bit of red rag attached. The greens were in the "rough", and the bunkers were in their natural state. If a player went off the narrow course of good ground he was at once landed in very "rough country", and the course at the ninth hole was all heathery and difficult, across its whole breadth.' These were the conditions that the first 'Greats' of golf, like Allan Robertson (b. St Andrews 1815), the golfball maker who was the first person to break 80 at St Andrews, had to deal with in refining the game.

Today, by far the most difficult and deceptive course to play is the Old. When the visiting golfer gazes down the first fairway — 367 yards of wide lawn — a deceptively easy shot is first suggested. But under the eagle eye of the 'knowledgeable old-parties' in the Royal & Ancient Golf Club's 'Big Room', his nerve begins to go. General Dwight D. Eisenhower knew the emotion well. On his first round at the Old Course in 1946, Eisenhower took a few practice shots at the First Tee, chickened out as he felt the gaze of the crowd on him and paced off to the Second Tee. Shamefaced, he admitted: 'If I whiffed on the first at St Andrews, I'd never live it down!'

As with the game of golf, the Old Course remains both enchanting and maddening. Sculpted largely by gale and tide over a period of 6000 years, the Old Course has slim fairways, once cropped to the earth by grazing sheep, and among the coverts of gorse there are traps for the unwary golfer in the tall spiky marram and sea lyme grasses. More than one hundred bunkers await the player; some are moonscaped pits, while others are small saucers just large enough to hold an apoplectic player and his niblick. Even the names of the bunkers intimidate — The Coffin, Hell, Grave and Lion's Mouth. But as he waits to play through, the golfer can enjoy the wide variety of plants — from the blue fleabane to the harefoot clover — which share the links with the six-spot Burnet Moth, the shelducks and the skylarks; and visitors can admire the yellow flowering tree-lupin, and enjoy the antics of linnets, yellow-hammers and warblers.

One much photographed and intriguing piece of architecture on the Old Course is the Swilcan Bridge near the 18th 'Tom Morris' Hole. This medieval bridge, in the spirit of the northcountry pack bridge, was once the only seaward link between the castle and cathedral with the Eden estuary, the early burgh harbour and the mussel beds.

To school the finest golfer, the Old Course is prone to perverse and illogically timed changes of weather. Some times the gales reach 60 mph here and golfers find their well struck ball arc-ing behind them. Many remember that this happened to Eric Brown, and others still recall that sunny day at the 1970 British Open when Neal Coles scored a record 65 (7 under par), while Tony Jacklin was 8 under par at the 13th. Then the calm day was drenched by a sudden downpour which inundated the links and the game was called off. Next day, with back bent against the wind and rain, Jacklin struggled through the last few holes in 3 under par: 'The Old Course got the last laugh,' he later philosophised to friends.

The earliest historical reference to golf in Scotland is found in the year 1457, when James II, King of Scots, forbade the playing of golf (and football) as it kept men away from their archery practice. The local Kirk Sessions were much against golf too, particularly in the sixteenth century, as it encouraged players to profane the Sabbath, and the very officers of the kirk were neglectful of their duties because of the game. Undoubtedly the earliest note of golf in St Andrews is dated 1552, when a grant of rights of warren on the links was agreed by Archbishop John Hamilton, guaranteeing the continuing of the rights of St Andreans to play golf on the links as well as 'futeball, shuting and all games, as well as casting divots, gathering turfs (for roofing)'. But the game was played elsewhere in Scotland as early as 1413.

Once the burghers of St Andrews rode ceremonially around the boundaries of the links to signify to the world the legality of their rights and the extent of their privileges; the ridings continued well into the nineteenth century. The links remained 'common ground' until they were exchanged by deed of excambion in part in 1763 with James Lumsden of Strathtyrum, and to Thomas Erskine, Earl of Kellie in 1797 and to George Cheape of Strathtyrum in 1848; but they were bought back for the town in 1893 and remain 'public property' via the Parliamentary Act of 1894.

Although the 'tyrannous game', as the poet R. F. Murray called it, was generally indulged most actively by the gentry, golf on the Old Course was free of charge to all comers, inhabitants and visitors alike until 1913, then a fee of 1/− (5p) was made for visitors. From 1912 to 1945 St Andrews ratepayers could play free, but in 1946 an annual subscription was imposed. Today the maintenance of the courses is in the hands of the Links Management Trust, what has been described as 'an oddly British institution' which had its birth in the act of parliament and the restructuring of local

General Dwight David Eisenhower (1890—1969), C-in-C Allied Forces in the European theatre of operations 1943—45, walks on to the first tee of the Old Course with R & A Captain Roger Weatherhead and deputy chairman of the R & A general committee Lt. Col J. Inglis, to play himself in as a honorary member of the R & A on Wednesday, 9 October 1946 (*The Estate of G. M. Cowie*).

government in 1974. It is made up of three members of the Royal & Ancient Golf Club, three members of North East Fife District Council, the sitting MP and the Secretary of State for Scotland. Since 1974 all the links have been owned by North East Fife District Council.

The tradition of golf in St Andrews gave rise to the Royal & Ancient Golf Club (commonly known as the 'R&A'), set overlooking the 1st and 18th tees of the Old Course. According to the records, on 14 May 1754, 22 noblemen and gentlemen of Fife formed themselves into 'The Society of St Andrews Golfers'. They all subscribed towards the purchase of a Silver Club to be played for annually over the links; and, the winner of the match was to be 'Captain of the Golf' for the ensuing year. The Silver Club continued to be played for until 1824, when it was decided to choose the Captain by personal merit alone. Today the R&A Captain still 'plays himself in' with a symbolic stroke at the 1st tee of the Old Course; the occasion takes place at 8 a.m. on the day of the Club's Annual Meeting and the Captain rewards the caddie who retrieves the ball with a gold sovereign. The caddies, whose skill can judge a Captain's potential, place themselves accordingly to retrieve the ball. It is recorded that when the Prince of Wales (later to be the Duke of Windsor) played himself in as Captain in 1922, the caddies 'stood disloyally near the tee'.

In 1834 King William IV accepted the invitation to become the Club's patron and thereafter the Club was designated 'Royal and Ancient'. Club meetings took place in the early days at a number of places in the town, from Glass's Inn to the Black Bull Tavern, and then in the Union Parlour on the site of the Grand Hotel (now Hamilton Hall students' residence). The present Clubhouse was built in 1854 and the R&A remains a private club of 1800 members who are all 'invited' to join. In 1897 the Club appointed its first Rules of Golf Committee, and from that date the R&A was recognised as 'Governing Authority for the Rules of Golf in all countries except the USA, Canada and Mexico' — the latter countries legislate their own rules, but in consultation with the R&A. The R&A conducts the Open and Amateur Championships, which were inaugurated in 1860 and 1885 respectively, and has done so since 1919. By 1888 the R&A had become the sole ruling body of the game. The first Open Championship to be played in St Andrews was in 1873. The R&A Clubhouse contains a multitude of 'golfing treasures', from portraits ranging from that of the longest surviving Captain of the Club in John Whyte-Melville of Bennochy and Strathkinness, who was a member for 60 years, to the portrait of the Prince of Wales of 1922. The Club also displays the old Dutch Master 'Ice on the Scheldt', attributed to Van Ostade, presented to the Club in 1949 by Robert Boothby, 1st Baron

Boothby, who was Rector of the University in 1958. Other treasures include cups, medals, trophies and clubs which belonged to famous golfers.

The earliest golf club to be founded in St Andrews, after the R&A, was the Thistle Golf Club which lasted in its first form from 1817 to 1838; this was a club for tradesmen and artisans and went into desuetude in 1839 but was re-formed in 1865 and still exists. The St Andrews Golf Club was instituted in 1843 as the golf club of the town's merchants and tradesmen too and this club was one of those which retained the red jacket 'uniform' for some years. One of the club's early captains was Allan Robertson, the world's first professional golfer. The New Golf Club was founded in 1902. The first golf club for women in the town was founded in 1867 (indeed, it was the first ladies' golf club in Scotland), and St Rule's Ladies Club was founded in 1898, while St Regulus Ladies Golf Club was founded before World War I.

Although the caddying business has declined since the introduction of caddie-carts in 1949 — the first caddying car to be wheeled over the Old Course was by the aviator and politician Baron Brabazon of Tara who died in 1964 — the caddies have remained a colourful lot. The name 'caddie', by the by, comes from the French *cadet* (junior), a word once used in Scotland to signify an 'errand boy'. With the decline of the fish trade in St Andrews, many of the old fishermen became caddies and added their pawky wit to caddy lore. Before World War I boy caddies were paid 1/6d (7½p) and men 2/6 (12½p) per round. As many caddies had caddied since they were boys they knew the finer points of the game. One such, George Smith McIntyre — nicknamed 'Sodger' — caddied for the Unionist Prime Minister 1915 — 16, A. J. Balfour, and remembered the politician consoling himself when he made a bad shot with the comment: 'If I always got what I wanted, I wouldn't play golf'. Other caddies made more caustic comments. Once when the Bishop of London whacked his ball out of the infamous Hell Bunker he said

'Out of Hell in one'. 'Aye, m'lord', said his caddy, 'and ye'd better tak the club wi' ye when ye dee.' The caddies still retain their own 'shelter' by the 18th green, dwarfed by the flagstaff once the mast of the famous windjammer *Cutty Sark*.

Golf personalities come and go, but the surname Morris will live on in golfing history. Old Tom Morris (1821 – 1908) was born in North Street and, following elementary education at Madras College, he became an apprentice to a golf ball manufacturer. Eventually he was appointed greenkeeper of the R&A in 1865 and he continued in this position until 1903. The burgh is still full of Morris-lore and Old Tom kept the St Andrews links in the premier position amongst British golf courses using the minimum of greenkeeping equipment (he began with a spade, a shovel and a barrow). It appears that Old Tom Morris began to play golf at the age of 6 and he went on to win the Open Championship four times – he failed to beat the celebrated Willie Park by one stroke in 1860 during his first ever Open. Eventually Old Tom was surpassed in skill by his son Young Tom Morris, who was a brilliant golfer of his day, and who won the Open Championship three times in a row to 1870. Young Tom died in 1875 at the early age of 24. Memorials to the two famous Morrises are to be found in the cathedral graveyard.

Many a skilled golfer in St Andrews began as a cleek-maker – that nineteenth century word for a golf-club based on the old Scots 'cleekit' meaning hooked. It is not known exactly when golf-club and -ball making was begun in St Andrews, but by 1672 the likes of James Pett was supplying such St Andrews *alumni* as James Graham, 1st Marquis of Montrose. 'Forgan is one of the best known names in the club-making trade, and wherever golf has penetrated, clubs turned out by this firm are to be found.' So one correspondent to the magazine *Golf Illustrated* commented about Messrs R. Forgan & Son in the early 1900s. Robert Forgan (1824 – 1900), who learned club-making from his uncle Hugh Philp (1782 – 1856), official club maker to the Society of Golfers, took over the latter's business in 1856; by 1890 he was

Tom Morris, Snr, was appointed greenkeeper and professional golfer to the R & A in 1865, and he retired from active duties as professional in 1904, aged 83. Born in St Andrews in 1821, Morris knew every aspect of the game of golf and was Open Champion four times, competing in every Open Championship from its institution in 1860 to 1896. The Home Green (the 18th hole) of the Old Course — which he was instrumental in laying out in its present form — was named in his memory.

employing fifty workmen. In 1863–64, when the then Prince of Wales was elected Captain of the R&A, Robert Forgan made him a set of clubs which won him the ultimate *imprimatur* to legend all his wares 'By Appointment to His Majesty King Edward VII'; the Prince of Wales feathers were impressed below the maker's name.

The firm's golfballs, the *Forgan* and *Acleva*, were favourites with golfers all over the world, and the firm boasted that they alone employed a man to hand-hammer golf balls to give them extra drive and straightness. Forgan's premises were situated on the modern site of the 'St Andrews Woollen Mill'. Robert Forgan, too, pioneered the use of the hickory shafts, and he bought his wood, from Quebec, at Dundee docks. In St Andrews the modern trade of golf-club making is carried on by such as J. B. Halley & Co Ltd, Slotline Golf Europe, and Swilken of St Andrews. For more than 200 years, it may be remembered, the only accepted golf ball was a 'featherie', a sphere packed with down, which dated from around 1618. Then in 1845, a St Andrean called Robert Paterson produced a ball of *gutta-percha*, only bettered by the rubber-covered ball of 1899, still in use today.

Another famous golf-club maker in St Andrews was Tom Stewart. Born in 1861, he was a skilled maker of horseshoes for Robert Hamilton who had his forge at the West Port. Stewart learned the art of club-making, though, from the blacksmith Robert White who had his forge at The Pends. By 1902 Stewart had opened his own forge in Greyfriars Garden but soon moved to the Argyle Factory. There he made his cleeks bearing the 'Pipe' brand (the clay pipe mark had been used by Stewart's brother John on his tools when working as a jute tenter) which went all over the world. Stewart retired and died in 1931 and his business was taken over in 1933 by A. G. Spalding & Bros who transferred production to Northern Ireland in 1963.

No comment on golf-club making in St Andrews would be complete without a mention of Laurie Auchterlonie. Son of Willie Auchterlonie, who won the Open in 1893, Laurie was born in 1904 and became honorary professional of the R&A like his father, and was a skilled clubmaker at his premises in Pilmour Links/Golf Place. His first museum collection of golf memorabilia was shipped to Pinehurst, North Carolina. He died in 1987 but his business survives.

And so golf goes on in St Andrews and always will while the ancient burgh exists, as George Fullerton Carnegie of Pitarrow wrote in 1813:

> And still St Andrews Links with flags unfurl'd
> Shall peerless reign, and challenge all the world.

CHAPTER 12

Modern St Andrews: A Personal Perspective

To my taste no other town in Scotland gives you the same amalgam of faith, assiduity, devotion, liberty and authority as a legacy as St Andrews, with all these factors enshrined in the legends of the little burgh. St Andrews is deep rooted and its life and times are set fast in Scottish myth and allusion. The best place to begin to view modern St Andrews is from the A918, St Andrews-Crail road, as it rises out of the town and above the swimming pool and leisure centre (1988); there 900 years of burgh development may be glimpsed in a moment where the craggy old 'Headland of the King's Mount' juts out into St Andrews Bay.

St Andrews looks impeccably the part of the small medieval burgh. As you follow the A918 down into the town you see how it lies infinitely solid and reliable as a place where you still make a positive effort to visit. There is no motorway thundering anywhere near and the nearest railway station is four miles away. Although we have seen that St Andrews has been a burgh since around 1144, it is hardly the centre of commercial bustle. The true focus of life in modern St Andrews is still the medieval old town and both tradesmen and residents feel the town is part of their very selves.

The burgh is a distinctly Scottish town of homegrown architectural traditions as befits a place that has always played an important rôle in the history of Scotland. The burgh has survived time, tide and weather and offers a network of wide streets, wynds, quads and leafy squares of honey-coloured medieval sandstone buildings which merge with the grey of Victorian and Edwardian architecture. There is a harmony here of seascape and landscape offering a cosy co-existence for college man and woman with burgess, and once for cleric. For the visitor the wynds — that lovely soothing

Personnel from RAF Leuchars parade down North Street to exercise their right as freemen of the burgh, with bayonets fixed and colours flying. On 24 August 1968 the airbase was granted the freedom of St Andrews in recognition of its services in peace and war and to mark the 50th anniversary of the RAF (*Royal Air Force*).

Scottish word for a lane leading off a main thoroughfare — in particular have much to offer in surprise views and a semi-private world of characterful buildings, flowers and trees.

And South Street offers the most wynds: there's Baker Lane with its sculpted crowned head of *circa* the fourteenth century, set into a gable end; there's Crail's Lane, wherein the burgh of Crail was assigned feus in 1517; there's the pantiled houses of Imrie's Close and Rose Lane; there's Ladebraes Lane with its high walls leading to the quiet cul-de-sac by Westview and leafy Queen's Terrace. And Abbey Court leading to the delightful theatre set in a re-sculpted lang rigg.

St Andrews has played a key rôle in the development of modern theatre in Scotland. The idea of a theatre in the Old Byre of the Abbey Street Dairy Farm was first conceived by Alexander Brown Paterson MBE. A journalist by profession, Alex Paterson was the theatre's administrator until he retired in 1980; he had been the theatre's resident playwright, actor and majordomo for over fifty years. The theatre was founded in 1933 and the guiding lights of the enterprise were members of the St Andrews Play Club which had been formed in embryo amongst members of the Hope Park Church Bible Class. Plays were performed in very spartan surroundings at the old Byre from 1933 — 36, then theatrical regulations had to be complied with, and after refurbishment a new performing licence was granted in 1937. Thereafter during summer the Play Club presented a repertoire of plays for both visitors and residents. Activities were called to a temporary halt when war broke out in 1939, but the Dundee Repertory Company were able to stage performances from time to time while their theatre was being reconstructed. The first St Andrews Repertory Company was formed in 1940 and somehow the theatre managed to keep open until the end of the war in 1945. In 1969 there was the final season of 'the Old Byre' and preparations were made for a new theatre opened by the late celebrated Scottish actor Andrew Cruickshank in 1970. Today the theatre flourishes for both professional and amateur shows tackling such plays of power and intensity as 'Diary of Anne Frank' (1982) and in 1988 the Byre transferred its production of 'The Miracle Worker' by

The wide expanse of South Street offers a diversity of architecture from the 16th to the 19th centuries. In the foreground is the Pends gateway (*circa* 1350) and the Roundel (*circa* 1590) with its balustraded parapet. South Street was the great medieval processional way to the cathedral, evolving from 1160. The street's distinctive lime trees date from 1879—80 (*Peter Adamson*).

William Gibson to the Westminster Theatre in London's Theatreland.

Although the population has swollen to 13,660 in 1988 from the 4590 of the late eighteenth century, St Andrews has changed little, except for the southward suburban sprawl, since the first attempts to depict the town by such as Captain John Slezer (d.1714) in *Theatrum Scotiae* (1693). This southern development evolved 1930—80 with the St Andrews abbatoir, opened in 1932 to replace the one in South Bridge Street, being the precursor of the tiny edge of town 'industrial estate'. It is easy for residents to be selfish about St Andrews, but for many the town is already 'too big' and the idea of a burgeoning southern aspect of St Andrews by Bogward or advancing up the hill at Pipeland to Wester Balrymonth is anathema. Only time will tell as to who wins and loses; the fear is that more houses mean more people, and more people mean more traffic, both of which will destroy the individuality of St Andrews' character.

Others see another monster waiting to be unchained, the expansion of the popularity of golf. In its restricted site on the Scores the world's governing body for golf, the R&A, sits and considers, all the time wishing to expand building complexes along the Scores and by the sea. Most of the townsfolk would range themselves against them in such plans to alter one of Scotland's most distinctive sites. And the people are likely to win as 'conservation' and 'preservation' are averred to be the watchwords of St Andreans in the 1990s. In the past St Andrews has been reasonably served by her publicly elected town councillors, with the odd bloomer of demolishing a fine old building, and the erection of a 'hideous monstrosity' here and there — the 'monstrosity' being filled in to suit personal taste.

After World War I there were to be some political changes affecting St Andrews. The Reform Act of 1918 brought St Andrews Burghs into the East Fife Constituency and there was to be some political controversy when Col. Sir Alexander Sprot, the Unionist candidate, defeated the ex-Liberal Prime

Minister H. H. Asquith (1852—1928) in December 1918; Sprot represented the seat until 1922. (Sir) James D. Millar, the Liberal Nationalist, held the constituency during 1922—24 and 1929—32, having been ousted from 1924 to 1929 by the Conservative, Commander the Hon. A. D. Cochrane. Sir James Henderson-Stewart, the National Liberal and Conservative, sat for East Fife from 1933—1961, and thereafter it was held by Sir John Gilmour until his retirement in 1979. The seat was held for the Conservatives again by Barry Henderson until 1983, whereupon the constituency became Fife North East and Henderson served 1983—87 until he was defeated by the Liberal lawyer Menzies Campbell. In terms of local government St Andrews is served by the Fife Regional Council, North East Fife District Council and the Community Council of which the former is Labour controlled and the latter two by the Liberals in their guise as the SLD. Emphasis is put publicly by these ruling groups on 'community affairs', but the dead hand of party politics is all too clear.

The St Andrews Preservation Trust is the watchdog on conservation and preservation work in the burgh. The Trust was founded in 1937, incorporated in 1938, and has the clearly defined object of securing 'the preservation of the amenities and historical character of St Andrews and its neighbourhood.' Preservation work had begun in earnest in the town in the eighteenth century, when through the prompting of the university, the Exchequer repaired St Rule's tower in 1789 and through the early nineteenth century a large portion of the castle, West Port, priory walls and cathedral were repaired.

Alas 'vandalism' was mixed with preservation as the medieval town kirk (Holy Trinity) was ruthlessly destroyed as was the medieval hall of St Salvator's college, and several other ancient architectural features. The Preservation Trust's museum at 12 North Street, within the old Ladyhead, by the by, contains exhibitions of a distillation of the town's history in the form of an old grocer's shop, an old chemist's shop, early postcards and photographs of St Andrews, and bygones of the town and ephemera of the fishing community. Incidentally, 12 North Street with its moulded doorway dates from 1619 and has a panelled hall; the house was renovated in 1937 and 1963. The Royal Burgh of St Andrews treasures are kept at the Town Hall, but there is limited public access to the displays. The chain of office worn by the provosts of St Andrews was presented to the burgh in 1897 by John-Patrick Crichton-Stuart (1847—1900), the 3rd Marquess of Bute.

Coastal erosion has always been a problem in St Andrews, and for hundreds of years succeeding town councils conducted a make-do-and-mend policy. In recent years though the existing sea wall along the worst stretch of erosion, the walkway by Prior Hepburn's Walls, overlooking the harbour, was buttressed to underpin the existing sea wall of 1856—57. Since medieval times as much as three feet of cliff has been swept away by the sea at any one time. The regular planting of *ammophilia areanaria*, known as marram grass, along the West Sands has helped the erosion by sea and wind.

It was the effects of World War II that drastically focused attention in St Andrews both socially and architecturally. The town received its first Air Raid Warning on Friday, 20 October 1939 and on 25 October 1940 the town received 'direct hits' from bombs in Westburn Lane, Kinnessburn, Greenside Dairy and Alison Place. Hardly a blitz but enough to sow the seeds of the spirit of a need for future conservation. The war gave St Andrews a chance to welcome strangers within her gates on a scale not seen since medieval times when students came from Belgium, Poland and France to study and make St Andrews one of the most cosmopolitan places in Christendom. For, interestingly enough, the town welcomed Poles again, but under very different circumstances.

Polish soldiers arrived in St Andrews in 1940 and caused something of a stir with their distinctive uniforms and cloaks, and the enthusiastic way they sang their way to Mass at St

The memorial fountain to Victorian novelist George Whyte-Melville on the site of the burgh's tolbooth (demolished 1862) and the mercat cross (removed 1768). The Royal Bank of Scotland was opened here in 1857 and the Bank of Scotland in 1971 (on the site of the British Linen Bank, 1903).

James's on The Scores. The soldiers were billeted in the hotels, church halls and private houses of the town and carried out duties as a part of the coastal defence garrison. Some of them continued their university education there. The Polish staff officers had their headquarters at Cupar and the Commander-in-Chief of the Polish Army in Scotland, General Wladyslaw Sikorski, had his main base at Forfar. Several of the Polish soldiers remained in the town and married local girls and their names are perpetuated in telephone book, and electoral register. Today a colourful mosaic panel in the wall of the Town Hall speaks of the gratitude of Polish soldiers who had received hospitality in the town during World War II.

The latest public building projects in St Andrews are the

This evocative picture, taken by the late Polish photographer 'Tad', shows Alexander Brown Paterson, MBE, taking a last look at the Old Byre Theatre in the old byre of the Abbey Street Dairy Farm, before its demolition in 1969; the old workshop is on the right and the theatre on the left. Founded in 1933, the theatre moved into its new premises in 1970. A journalist by profession, A. B. Paterson served as the theatre's administrator until 1980 (*A. B. Paterson*).

development of the £1.7 million British Golf Museum on The Scores at Bow Butts on the site of office accommodation used by the St Andrews Links Trust. The original plans for the museum caused much controversy in the town when first mooted by the R&A and a single-storey building was ultimately agreed. Including 6500 sq feet of exhibition space the building will be faced in Clasach sandstone from

Morayshire and will be built into the Bow Butts to retain the magnificent views of the Angus coast. This project's neighbour is the £750,000 Sea Life Centre newly constructed on the site of the Step Rock Pool bathing station; the Centre was opened on 15 June 1989 by HRH The Duchess of York.

And whither St Andrews? The seagulls will continue to wheel and dive over the town; the red gown will remain as a symbol of learning; and the towers of St Rule and St Salvator will survive to dominate the landscape, for no skyscrapers will be built here. Will they? Perhaps a clue to the future of old St Andrews is seen in the timeless permanence of the ruins of Blackfriars in South Street, a fragment when Scotland's modern history was being made. For today the heart of the town would be recognised by Johnson and Boswell, Scott and Lang as the place they knew. But what of the town's extremities? Developers circle like wolves seeking to expand into the fields around St Andrews. Will they succeed? One certainty is that St Andrews will continue the evolution from university city into holiday resort and further into golf mega-city as the slow dominance of the 'tyrannising game' swamps all else. Already myriad folk come to play golf at St Andrews who never enter the old town to shop or just to stare. Once St Andrews was the centre of civilised Scotland, but is her future now tied in solely to the erratic trajectory of a little white ball?

Further Reading

It is always my intent to present readers with suggestions for further reading by listing books that are reasonably available in libraries rather than those which are only available to the specialist. I have already mentioned the seminal and earliest histories of the town by George Martine of Claremont (*Reliquiae Divi Andreae*, 1797), Rev. J. C. Lyon (*History of St Andrews*, 1843) and James Grierson (*Delineation of St Andrews*, 1807), and would offer the following as supplementary reading:

Town
BRUCE, G. *Wrecks & Reminiscences of St Andrews Bay*, 1884.
FREW, J. (Ed). *Building for a New Age*, n.d.
Georgian and Early Victorian St Andrews, 1946. St Andrews Preservation Trust.
KIRK, R. *St Andrews*, 1954.
LAMONT-BROWN, R. *St Andrews City of Change*, 1984.
LAMONT-BROWN, R. *A Visitors Guide to St Andrews & The East Neuk*, 1985.
ROBERTSON, E. S. *Old St Andrews*, 1923.
St Andrews: The Preservation Trust Guide and History, 1982.
YOUNG, D. *St Andrews*, 1969.

Gown
CANT, R. G. *The College of St Salvator*, 1950.
CANT, R. G. *The University of St Andrews*, 1970.
DUNLOP, A. I. (ed.) *Acta Facultatis Artium Universitatis Sanctiandree*, 1964.
Handbook of St Mary's College, St Andrews, 1946.
HERKLESS, J. & HANNAY, R. *The College of St Leonard*, 1905.
MAITLAND ANDERSON, J. *Early Records of the University of St Andrews*, 1926.

TWISS, G. P. & CHENNELL, P. *Famous Rectors of St Andrews*, 1982.

University of St Andrews, Prospectus.

Cathedral & Priory
BAXTER, J. H. *Copiale Prioratus Sanctiandree*, 1930.
CRUDEN, S. *St Andrews Cathedral*, 1986.
FLEMING, D. H. *St Andrews Cathedral Museum*, 1931.
McROBERTS, D. (Ed). *The Medieval Church of St Andrews*, 1976.

Castle
CRUDEN, S. *St Andrews Castle*, 1982.

Golf
BRICKMAN, E. *et al. The Royal and Ancient Golf Club of St Andrews*, 1984.
ROBERTSON, J. K. *St Andrews Home of Golf*, 1984.

Newspapers
ST ANDREWS CITIZEN (1870–   ); ST ANDREWS GAZETTE (1914–15); ST ANDREWS GAZETTE & FIFE-SHIRE NEWS (1863–1883); ST ANDREWS TIMES (1937–1940).
Copies held by University of St Andrews Library, and St Andrews Public Library.

As a starting point, however, for a more detailed examination of St Andrews, I would suggest a look at the *Collection Towards A Bibliography of St Andrews* (1926) by Regius Professor of Ecclesiastical History J. H. Baxter.

Maps
c.1580s. *S. Andre sive Andreapolis Scotiae Universitas Metropolitana*. Reproduced as a frontispiece in *The Medieval Church of St Andrews* (1976).

1642. James Gordon, Minister of Rothiemay, Banff (d.1686). Pen and ink drawing of town seen from the north looking south. Reproduced in *Bannatyne Miscellany* (vol iii, p. 324, 1855).

1775. John Ainslie.

1807. J. Williams and D. Duff. Plan in *Delineation of St Andrews*. The 1838 edition contains a map by W. H. Lizars.

1820. J. Wood's Town Atlas.

1832. Report on Parliamentary Boundaries.

1843. The Rev. C. J. Lyon's *History of St Andrews* contains a poor copy by S. Leith of the c.1580s map in Vol. I. Vol II contains a plan of 1843 and a ground plan of the cathedral.

1988. Street Plan. St Andrews Merchants Association.

Index

Abbey Cottage, 31
Acca, Bishop of Hexham, 12, 13
Adamson, Dr John, 81, 160, 176
Alexander I, 17, 18, 39
Alexander III, 58
Anderson, Dr Elizabeth G., 152-53
Anderson, J. M., 180
Anderson, M. ('Cynicus'), 149
Angus I, king, 9, 10, 12, 13, 14
Angus, Fr George, 138, 140
Archbishops of St Andrews:
    Patrick Adamson, 70
    Cardinal David Beaton, 22, 45, 46,
    51-54, 116, 127-28
    James Beaton, 45, 51, 106, 116
    John Douglas, 142
    Andrew Forman, 51
    George Gledstanes, 56
    Patrick Graham, 51, 128
    John Hamilton, 45, 47, 54, 75, 106,
    116, 121, 188
    Arthur Rose, 48
    William Schevez, 42
    James Sharp, 78, 83, 139, 143, 144-45,
    180
    John Spottiswoode, 56, 76
    Alexander Stewart, 41, 51, 109, 112
    James Stewart, 40-41
Argyle, 60
Arnold, Abbot of Kelso, 24, 33, 34
Atholl Hotel, 121
Auchterlonie, L., 194-95
Auchterlonie, W., 185, 194
Augustinian Priory, 1, 11, 13, 18-29, 49,
    74, 92, 102, 112, 156, 207

Baldwin, Stanley, Prime Minister, 100,
    119
Balliol, John, 49, 58
Balnacarron, 4
banks, 171-72, 203
Barrie, Sir J. M., 100, 122, 167
Bassaguard (Bess Acre), 81
Bell, Adam, 160
Bell, Dr Andrew, 129, 146, 147
Bell, Dr Oswald H., 176

Benedict XIII (Pope), 94
Bishops of St Andrews:
    Arnold, 33, 34
    William Bell, 42
    David de Bernham, 141
    James de Bone, 49
    Cellach, 14
    Cellach II, 14
    Eadmer, 17
    Fothad II, 14, 16, 38
    William Frazer, 40
    Gamelin, 36, 40
    de Gullane, 36
    James Kennedy, 37, 42, 57-58, 95, 99,
    104-10, 128
    William de Lamberton, 20, 24, 36, 38,
    40, 49
    William de Landells, 42, 70
    William Malvoisin, 34, 36, 49, 126
Black Bull inn, 161, 190
Blue, Donald (James McDonald), 182
Blue Stane, 165
Boarhills, 5, 13, 50, 84, 162
Booth, Gen. Wm., 182
Boswell, James, 78, 132, 205
Boyd, Rev. A. K. H., 140, 143
Brewster, Sir David, 124, 136, 160
bridges, 81, 86, 187
Bruce, George, 84, 91, 176
Buchan, John, 167
Buchan, Lady, 80
Bute, 3rd Marquess of, 98, 120, 138, 168,
    173, 202
Byre Theatre, 198-99, 204

Campbell, Prior Alexander, 45
Campbell, Prof. Lewis, 152, 154
Canonical Hours, 23-26
Carnegie, Andrew, 117, 118; wife, 120
Carters/Whiplickers, 164-65
castle, 49-58, 70, 78, 207; bottle dungeon,
    50, 54; countermines, 54, 55
cathedral, 24, 28, 33-48, 78, 207;
    museum, 1, 2-3, 20, 40, 180, 207
céli dé (Culdees), 6-8, 18, 27, 92, 109, 112
Charles I, 68

209